W9-BZM-452

HOW *NOT* TO Hire

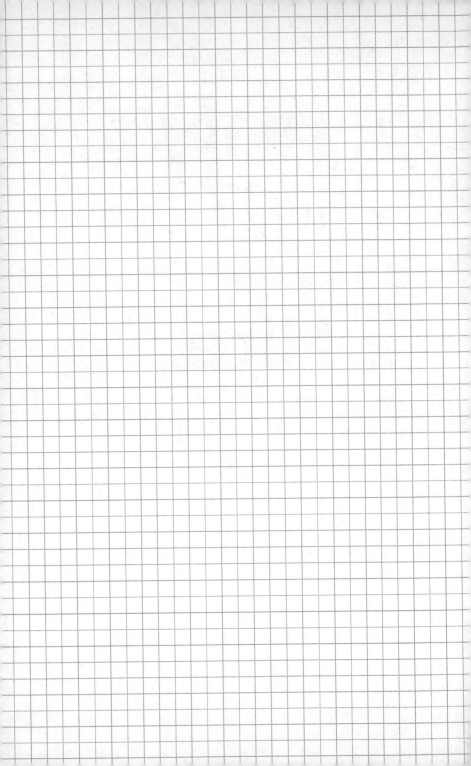

HOW
NOT
TO
Hire

Common mistakes to avoid
when building a team

Emily Kumler

HarperCollins
Leadership

An Imprint of HarperCollins

© 2020 HarperCollins Leadership

Published by HarperCollins Leadership, an imprint of HarperCollins Focus LLC.

Published in association with Kevin Anderson & Associates: https://www.ka-writing.com/.

Book design by Aubrey Khan, Neuwirth & Associates.

ISBN 978-1-4002-1969-8 (eBook)
ISBN 978-1-4002-1866-0 (HC)

Library of Congress Control Number: 2020936144

Printed in the United States of America
20 21 22 23 LSC 10 9 8 7 6 5 4 3 2 1

Contents

Section 1
The Search

Section 2
The Interview

Section 3
The Hire

A Special Dedication

This book is dedicated to the next generation of rascals: Max, Camilla, Charlotte, James, Ben, Arlo, Jude, Chloe, Charlie, Violet L, Henry, Etta, Sidney, Sydney, Thomas, Sam, Max, Cat, Violet M., Quinn, Em, Kai, Finley, Kavi, Jack, Teddy, and the little Kaplan on the way. I hope you always find the perfect balance of grit and perseverance, mixed with heavy doses of love and kindness, so that you may continue to evolve and always feel the support around you. May your lives be filled with meaningful mistakes that inspire deep learning and growth. My heart will always hold a special place for each of you. My arms are always free to hug you when you fall, and my mind is always here to help you strategize when you're ready to get back up and grow. I cannot wait to see the path each of you takes.

To Sandy, Marci, Carrie, and Natalie, thank you for holding space for me and keeping me grounded in all our worlds!

A special thank-you to Katy, Doug, Anne, Nicola, Jessie, Jessica, Payal, Lindsey, Jason, Kate TR, Harley, Ames, and big Camilla. I am acutely aware that every time I have fallen, broken in two, and wanted to hide in a pit of doom, you've come into the darkness, found me, held my hand, and shared in my sorrow. Then you've carefully and gently encouraged me, reminding me to get back up, to keep trying, to be true to my ideas. Risk-taking is less risky when you know you have an incredible crash pad. Failure doesn't feel so final when friends unrelentingly believe you'll find a way, maybe not the way you thought, but that you'll find a way to solve the problem. I'm endlessly grateful for your love and encouragement. Without it I would surely be a different person.

To my children, who in the span of three summer months survived their mother's mania: writing *two* books, hosting a weekly podcast, running three businesses, and venturing to Peru for two weeks. Thank you for inspiring me to get so much done! You two are the brightest lights in my life and have made me realize time is not something to take for granted. Who we spend our time with and how we spend it are by far the most important choices we make in life, a lesson you both have driven home for me. I am a better mom because of my passion for my work, and I'm a better worker because of my love for my family. I hope you will find your own balance and harmony, and perhaps even find that my example was helpful. Always remember: no matter where you go, no matter what you do, I will always love you. Oh, and I love you more. (Now that that is in print, I think we can agree it's official.)

To Mom, Dad, Kate, Dave, Aden, Marge, George, Robin, Michael, Billy, and Greta for being my family.

And to Bobby, my great love, who has constantly had to deal with my unsolicited advice. Your drive and intellect are unmatched. Your determination to find the truth, to question everything, to pursue the unpopular, inspires me every day. I'm deeply indebted that you're on this journey with me. Thank you for giving me the space and freedom to pursue what I believe matters. Your opinions are always the ones I value most. When we don't agree, I know it means I'm about to learn something important because your thoughtfulness is always revealing to me. And nothing is more validating than having your support and love. Thank you for sharing this life with me. I love you.

Introduction

You've probably seen the books that prescribe a path to success. Ones with titles like *10 Things You Must Do to Be Successful* and *Landing the Sale Every Time*. These books are a lot like fortune cookies—generic, obvious, and frankly, filled with hindsight bias. A look back at some of the best-selling self-help books of the past decades will lead you to a plethora of "success stories," which today are viewed as horror stories. Cherry-picked examples of profiled companies offer modern readers a glimpse into the likes of Enron, Lehman Brothers, and other now-defunct companies once touted as shining examples we mere mortals should try to emulate.

What I intend to do here is the opposite. Like most women in their forties, I've learned that the path to success must be defined by the individual. There are far too many variables in life to be pre-packaged into a perfect formula that will guarantee success. Most of the fortune-cookie books describe the need for grit, perseverance, and drive as their secret weapon. But look at almost any black, single mother in America, and I guarantee she's got grit, perseverance, and drive in spades that doesn't guarantee her a C-suite position. Like it or not, the bias and prejudice of the real world is a variable few self-help books consider when they're offering up their magical recipe for success.

> ∨ *Like it or not, the bias and prejudice of the real*
> ∨ *world is a variable few self-help books consider when*
> ∨ *they're offering up their magical recipe for success.*

I agree that many of the commonalities in those formulas are important, but in isolation they're not going to miraculously make you a millionaire, as some have suggested. Instead, we can take a realistic view of our options and consider what we know *doesn't* work and therefore what can be avoided, which I think is actually useful advice.

After two decades of reporting on business leaders, innovators, and criminals, it's clear to me that a lot of life's outcomes have to do with the lot *you* were handed. However, there are common pitfalls that can prevent you from achieving your personal potential if you're not cognizant of them. You'll look back on mistakes that hampered your pursuits and want a do-over. What if someone gave you a road map to those mistakes? Wouldn't that be better than generic advice on what you should do?

This book is about hiring people. We will assume you're reading this because you're in a position where you're hiring people, which means you're in a position of power. You now have a responsibility to hire the right people for the right roles. This sounds easy enough, right? But, actually it's an area of any business that can make or break the future, so wouldn't it be great to know mistakes others have made so you don't fall into the same trouble? That's my goal: to help you learn what not to do.

This book is not a legal guide to hiring; it is instead filled with stories of mistakes people have made and hardships they've faced in the hiring process. Each chapter offers different advice about hiring from the initial job posting to interviewing to offering a candidate a job. The stories are a mixture of reported, true stories and of amalgamations of my own experiences and those experiences I've heard about in my time working as an entrepreneur, speaker, and journalist. In those composite stories where I've taken the liberty to blend stories, to make up characters and details, the subjects are only referenced by their first names* in order to help the reader decipher between the accurate accounts and the fictionalized accounts. Those should not be confused with the stories of Cindy Brown, Emily Chang, Doug Levine, and Doug Stone who bravely shared their stories in interviews for this book in hopes of helping you all avoid the same pitfalls. All other stories are fictionalized portrayals of stories I've rendered from real life.

It is important to reiterate that each state has its own laws around hiring practices, and those are important to consult. This book only discusses laws and regulations in an anecdotal manner intended to highlight how rules change, what barriers are present, and how savvy businesspeople adapt. I believe there is much more to learn from people making mistakes or missteps than there is trying to isolate what worked. My intention is to entertain you with stories that will inform your own hiring practices and make you better, smarter, and more efficient at finding and keeping the best employees possible.

- ∨ *The stories are a mixture of reported, true stories*
- ∨ *and of amalgamations of my own experiences and*
- ∨ *those experiences I've heard about in my time*
- ∨ *working as an entrepreneur, speaker, and journalist.*
- ∨ *In those composite stories where I've taken the*
- ∨ *liberty to blend stories, to make up characters and*
- ∨ *details, the subjects are only referenced by their first*
- ∨ *names* in order to help the reader decipher between*
- ∨ *the accurate accounts and the fictionalized accounts.*
- ∨ *Those should not be confused with the stories of*
- ∨ *Cindy Brown, Emily Chang, Doug Levine, and Doug*
- ∨ *Stone who bravely shared their stories in interviews*
- ∨ *for this book in hopes of helping you all avoid the*
- ∨ *same pitfalls. All other stories are fictionalized*
- ∨ *portrayals of stories I've rendered from real life.*

When I was at Northwestern working toward my master's in journalism, I decided to take a business course. I wasn't a "math person" but I had a hunch that being familiar with financial reporting would come in handy when I was out of school and working as an investigative reporter. Our first assignment in that class was to write up an earnings report from a publicly traded Chicago-based corporation. My professor spent the first week painstakingly teaching us which elements of the report were most important and what to listen for on the investor call with the company. I did all that. Yet, when I sat down to file my story, I was lost. What was the difference between revenue and profit? Why was the P/E ratio important to a stock's value? Why did it seem like everyone else knew this stuff when none of it was familiar to me in any way?

My boyfriend had an MBA. I called him in a panic. He walked me through the balance sheet and income statement and then said, "So wait, you're writing this up and it's going to be printed in the papers tomorrow?" It was a terrifying idea. My work might be published, and the markets might respond to what I wrote? That felt wholeheartedly irresponsible, yet totally possible because all of the writing went out on the Medill News Service and could get picked up by any of the local papers.

Thank god that's not what happened. I failed the assignment. My assignment went nowhere. Despite my boyfriend's best efforts, my write-up sucked.

I had never *ever* gotten an F. Immediately, I looked into the add-drop guidelines: Was it too late to quit? Graduating Medill at the top of my class was important to me. I couldn't afford to chance it all on some business reporting class that might risk tanking my average.

My professor seemed to know what I was going to say as soon I began and interrupted me: "Wait, wait, you are perfectly within your rights to be concerned," he said. "You don't seem to have a handle on corporate filings at all. However, you're hardly someone who seems to shy away from challenges based on your lively contributions to our in-class discussions."

It sounded like he was calling me a dumbass and complimenting me at the same time. "I have no experience with business reporting, and it seems like everyone else does," I said. "And, frankly, I have no understanding of how these numbers relate to each other, I have to look everything up every time because they don't make any sense to me. I know there's a relational quality to these reports, but it is like reading a foreign language to me. I thought this would be a great chance to learn, but I seem to be way behind already."

"You are. That's all correct," he said.

"I took economics in college and loved it, but I've never had any interest in accounting," I said, hoping to explain that I liked the big-picture stuff, but would prefer to leave the detailed work to others (I was young and naive, forgive me).

"Yes, well, you can't really have one without an understanding of the other," he said.

"I grew up on the *Wall Street Journal*, but I never read the stock pages," I continued with my analogies, trying to delicately say: *I like the idea of business, but the numbers make me uneasy.*

"Emily, I think I'm known as a tough, but fair grader. Your final grade is based on ten earnings reports, four features, two profiles. You can write as many as you want of any of these and I will drop your lowest grades. So, if you think you can improve, write more and your average will improve—assuming you do indeed get better."

In my mind, the conversation had been about gracefully explaining that this class wasn't for me, but then I recognized the challenge he was putting forward. If I could figure out these corporate filings, I could write eleven earnings reports, and that F would be erased. I've always been a sucker for a good challenge.

Needless to say, my grades didn't go from that F to an A in one assignment. After more than twenty-five earnings reports, I got it. I worked my ass off in that class. There is little doubt that I turned in more stories, perhaps by a factor of two, than my classmates. In the end, I was the only one to get an A that quarter in the econ class. I still use that experience to remind myself, more than fifteen years later, that sometimes the thing that feels like it will undo me, or derail my plans, or is too hard is going to be the thing that propels me more than anything else.

> ∨   *I still use that experience to remind myself, more*
> ∨   *than fifteen years later, that sometimes the thing*
> ∨   *that feels like it will undo me, or derail my plans, or is*
> ∨   *too hard is going to be the thing that propels me*
> ∨   *more than anything else.*

I started out not knowing and I made tons of mistakes, but I stuck with it and learned from my errors. I ended up graduating from Medill with the best job offer in my class, and it was a business reporting gig. I never would have gotten that job had I not stuck with it and dialed in on my weaknesses with the support of a wonderful teacher. That's one example of learning how the wrong way teaches us the right way, if you can bear with it. You need to work hard, you need to be determined, and you need to be driven, but sometimes you also need to know what doesn't work and understand why it doesn't work. Feeling the sting of failure can motivate you to address the areas you're not good at, which is an incredible opportunity to make yourself better in profound ways. It is just as useful, if not more, to know the wrong way to do something than it is to be told exactly how to do it, because the other truth here is that there are infinite ways to be successful, but there are often very specific ways to fail.

I actually hate the word *failure*. It has a feeling of finality, which is misleading. Failure is not the end, it is often just the beginning of a growth period. That is why I've picked sources in this book who have failed and learned from their experiences. You too will fail. And, hopefully, you will have the opportunity to learn from your failures and grow. This book will tell you ways you *might* fail in hopes of preempting those moments and preventing them. We will look at these examples of failure from real people and amalgamations of stories I've heard or experienced over the years. I hope my writing transcends these tales in a way that allows you to learn from our mistakes.

   ∨   *I actually hate the word* failure. *It has a feeling of*
   ∨   *finality, which is misleading. Failure is not the end, it*
   ∨   *is often just the beginning of a growth period. That is*
   ∨   *why I've picked sources in this book who have failed*
   ∨   *and learned from their experiences. You too will fail.*
   ∨   *And, hopefully, you will have the opportunity to learn*
   ∨   *from your failures and grow.*

HOW
NOT
TO
Hire

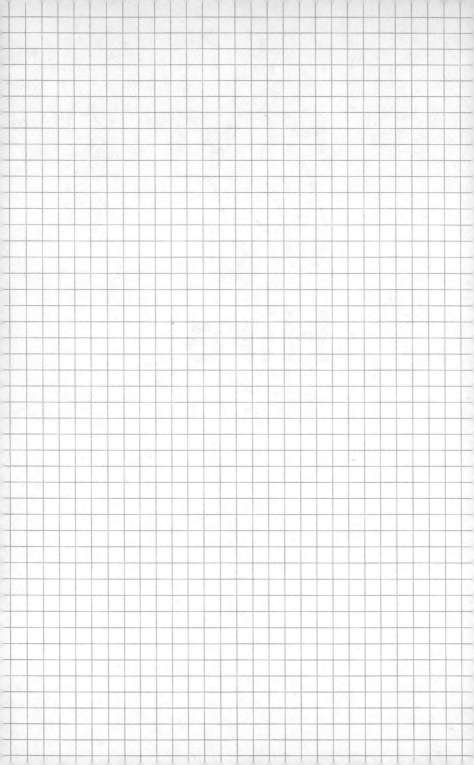

The Search

Hiring is a little like dating, you hope for the best but prepare for the worst. Just like the hunt for a mate, the best way to screw things up is to be disingenuous about your needs and their interests. Once upon a time, I stumbled upon a close friend's online dating profile. She was gorgeous, brilliant, and tons of fun. But she was not the avid football fan that she claimed to be—it's probably safe to say anyone who calls themselves an *avid* football fan is likely not. Nor was she any good at flip cup. Her profile was filled with things she was not. It was clear she was describing what she thought guys would want: a beer-guzzling, football-loving, hot chick, but this begs the question: What would happen when they found out who she actually was, an art-loving homebody who hated beer?

The same phenomenon happens with hiring. We all want to connect and like each other, and sometimes that means we're not 100 percent honest about what we're looking for or what we're offering. But, you actually need to be brutally honest about what you need in the role you're hiring for or you will end up with a candidate who doesn't work out. You must know your organization's culture, structure, and its needs before you can bring on an all-star that will be the perfect fit for your business.

> ✓ *You actually need to be brutally honest about what*
> ✓ *you need in the role you're hiring for or you will end*
> ✓ *up with a candidate who doesn't work out. You must*
> ✓ *know your organization's culture, structure, and its*
> ✓ *needs before you can bring on an all-star that will be*
> ✓ *the perfect fit for your business.*

Making a hiring decision is a big investment. Significant time and capital go into training new employees and it is all a big waste if you pull a bait-and-switch because when they learn what you're really all about, they'll be looking for another job and you'll be looking for their replacement. Or worse still, you bring on someone you're impressed by who doesn't have any of the necessary skills and you reveal your own shortcomings as a manager.

Defining your search is the key to your success. If my friend had described her love for travel, art, and literature, she might have met her match much sooner. If you need an admin, but you list the position as creative director, you too will have a drawn-out, more frustrating experience.

Think about what responsibilities your hire will have, then ask yourself what kinds of people tend to be good at those sorts of tasks and who tends to be bad at them.

Reverse engineer the hiring process starting with what you don't want. Asking yourself who would be terrible in the role is an incredibly valuable exercise that hardly anyone does. Consider the inverse: what you don't want. It might help you eliminate candidates earlier in your process, saving you time and advancing your quest for the right person.

If you need someone to manage your calendar, pick up your dry cleaning, do background research for upcoming client meetings, and file your bills, you're not looking for someone who shows up late or too early to the interview. If anyone walks in with a disheveled suit, send 'em packing. You need to trust that the hire is responsible, organized, and a Type-A, detail-oriented machine. If they don't own an iron, they might not be your best option. Likewise, someone who has spent the last three summers in Europe might not be down for your two-weeks-per-year vacation policy. These are important factors for long-term success in the position and within the company.

Imagine someone you know who would be perfect for the job and make a list of the qualities that made them come to mind, then look for others with those characteristics.

When you're hiring on behalf of someone else, it is essential to understand how the role and ideal candidate looks in the eyes of that specific boss. Get the details right from the beginning, and you'll be able to search for those specifics. Ask lots of questions. Maybe even spend a day shadowing someone who's currently kicking butt in that role. The more you know about what's required to be successful in the position, the more likely you'll be able to match it to someone who will thrive.

∨   *When you're hiring on behalf of someone else,*
∨   *it is essential to understand how the role and ideal*
∨   *candidate looks in the eyes of that specific boss.*
∨   *Get the details right from the beginning, and you'll*
∨   *be able to search for those specifics. Ask lots of*
∨   *questions. Maybe even spend a day shadowing*
∨   *someone who's currently kicking butt in that role.*

A lot like a reporter trying to get the story, you're looking to get to know people in a short period of time, which is made more difficult by laws and practices that prevent you from asking many questions. For example, you may know the role is intense, and when employees miss work, it is especially detrimental to the whole team, but you cannot ask if they've missed a lot of work in the past or any questions about their health. So instead of asking questions, I recommend setting clear expectations like: *This is a super intense position, members of the team rarely call in sick and most schedule vacations around project breaks. This is something you should consider, as it's not the lifestyle everyone wants.* This gives the candidate a chance to think honestly about the commitments required to perform in the position. It is always better to have someone back out of the application because they realize they cannot perform in the job than it is to hire them and be faced with having to fire them for underperforming. Saving that time and getting to the heart of it saves money and productivity down the line.

You are tasked with gaining keen insights in an extremely short period of time to make an important decision with a limited data set. Listening carefully and following up properly will help you immensely. Finding areas to expand upon in the interview, with references, and even when the candidate is first hired is essential to successfully hiring the right people for the right jobs.

One of the most common mistakes people fall into in hiring is the modern idea that a candidate for a job must already have the skills required to do the job. Relying on algorithms to search for candidates with specific skills is a recent phenomenon that greatly limits the talent pool. Until recently, we looked for people with an interest and the ability to learn. If you find someone who doesn't yet know how to do the job, but who really wants to learn, they may become one of your best workers because you've given them an opportunity that allows them to grow. Most people want jobs that are fulfilling in some way. Hiring someone who already knows everything about the job may seem great, but it may also mean that the new employee is bored and looking for another job sooner than you may want.

If your search is flawed, then your hiring will be off. Consider who you're looking for, what the candidates are looking for, and the skills they need versus the ones you can teach them. Search in an open and honest way, and you'll be way ahead of the pack.

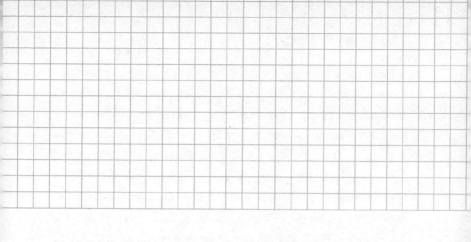

ONE

Only Look for Candidates Who *Already* Have the Skills Needed to Perform the Job

Technology companies used to train their employees to do the work the company needed, rather than hiring people who already had the skills to do the work. Today, we've shifted to a hiring environment that looks exclusively for people with the right skills. In much the same way that algorithms present problems because their parameters are limited to the data sets that they're trained on, so too are we entrenched in a hiring modality that prioritizes skills over abilities.

In 2016, Byron Auguste, the co-founder and president of Opportunity@Work, told a group at an MIT conference how an inclusive employment approach changed the course of his family's life. I was in the audience and realized our country's hiring problem is almost philosophical. As he explained, at our core we've changed from a landscape that taught workers the skills they needed, to one that expects workers to show up already trained, and then we complain when we can't find qualified people to hire.

Auguste's personal story was indicative of the 1970s when tech companies were eager to grow, but very few people knew how to work with computers. He told us his father answered an advertisement in the newspaper calling for anyone interested in learning COBOL, a computer programing language, to attend a workshop. The government, working with IBM, was offering a paid training program for anyone willing to develop this new skill. His father signed up, learned the language, loved it, and was soon employed by IBM, changing his family's future forever.

His talk focused on how today there are thousands of people in inner cities and throughout the Rust Belt that could easily learn to code—filling a much-needed void in the market. Training Americans, just like his father, would help disenfranchised workers achieve upward mobility in the workplace. It would also allow tech companies to build their talent pools.

There has been a lot of talk about American jobs going overseas, that international trade deals have negatively impacted the job market, but this only looks at the issue as an exclusive perspective rather than considering an inclusive approach. What if the labor problems in the United States are due to a lack of training for the jobs that are in demand rather than a lack of *overall* jobs?

We tend to forget that labor markets are at their essence just markets. They follow the same rules of supply and demand as any other market. Why do we spend so much money screening out the people who do not have the qualities we desire rather than spending that same money on training people to have the skills we need? We have loads of people out of work who once handled the demands of the manufacturing sector. Now that those jobs are mostly automated by machines, we no longer have the demand for the people. But, we have a huge demand for people who know how to build, design, and manage machines, so wouldn't it be logical to invest in teaching people those tech skills?

In his lecture at MIT, Auguste explained that since the 1970s, there's been a dramatic shift in our institutional training programs. It's estimated that workers receive 30 percent less training per capita than they did forty years ago. Our economy has shifted from an inclusive workforce, where evaluations were based on the question, "Can you learn to do this?" to an exclusive environment, where the question is, "Do you already know how to do this?" And if the answer to that last question is "no" then you're discarded and considered unqualified. Society often views minimum wage as a safety net for the poorest workers, but our human capability and our ability to learn new skills is perhaps the best safety net—if people are willing to train us. Teaching people the skills that are in demand will advance the individual and bring new prosperity to the nation as a whole. And, neglecting to recognize the potential of those looking for work is equally impactful. "In misjudging the potential of these workers, we not only undermine our civic values of fairness and equality of opportunity; we also lose the additional work, wages, ideas and improvements they would otherwise have created, contributed, and earned," Auguste wrote in *Forbes* in 2019.[1]

In our current, exclusive hiring approach, we search for keywords that match skills needed in the jobs we're trying to fill. We might set up an online advertisement that lists the qualifications for the position. But we're actually listing the skills of the people who are currently doing that job rather than the abilities required to learn how to do that job.

When many industries feel the hardships of a limited talent pool, why aren't we more open-minded in our recruiting efforts? Instead of requiring someone to already have all the skills, look for people who are eager to learn those skills. In many cases the current model excludes candidates who would thrive in the roles by preferentially deferring to those with more skills or credentials. The extension of that is, when we hire people who already know how to do every aspect of the job, they are more likely to be bored, frustrated, under-stimulated—they're not learning much. But when hungry candidates who do not already possess all the necessary skills get the job, they hit the ground running because they're eager to acquire those skills.

They will also be grateful you've invested in them. Your confidence in their ability to learn and your trust that they can do the job will make the worker feel a sense of appreciation and loyalty towards you and the organization. Whereas, someone who's a plug-and-play candidate won't feel as much long-term gratitude. They may not be as hungry to learn.

> ∨ *When many industries feel the hardships of a limited*
> ∨ *talent pool, why aren't we more open-minded in our*
> ∨ *recruiting efforts? Instead of requiring someone to*
> ∨ *already have all the skills, look for people who are*
> ∨ *eager to learn those skills.*

Key Takeaways

When you find yourself feeling frustrated that the labor market is too tight and you cannot find anyone to fill your job openings, remind yourself that the labor market is just that, a *market*, ruled by the laws of supply and demand.

- If you have a demand that cannot be fulfilled, figure out how you can increase the supply.
- If you need people who can do a specific thing—whatever that is—consider offering a training program that would build your supply of qualified workers.
- You'll have a pool of people who now have the exact skills you desire, and furthermore, you'll be able to evaluate that pool and select the top candidates for your positions.
- When you go to hire your next employee, think about the abilities you desire rather than skills that will be utilized in the position, and you will see your talent pool expand in wonderful ways.

TWO

Trust the Data and Rely Exclusively on Algorithms to Find *Your* People

Finding the right candidates who meet your needs is the million—or billion—dollar mission of many recruiting companies and online platforms. Platforms from Indeed to LinkedIn to HeadHunter, it seems, use artificial intelligence as the default way to look for job candidates. This part of the hiring process is very much entrenched. It is not the future, it is our reality. But it's hardly a perfect system.

Understanding the shortcomings of AI includes understanding how the algorithms are developed. All searches yield candidates who fit certain criteria. This is not like, "I need someone who can type," it is far more robust than that. Algorithms are trained on old data sets. In other words, we're programming the future with inputs from the past. Which means if you're hoping to break old patterns—because you're looking for a more diverse or gender-balanced workforce—you'll be hard-pressed to find an inclusive algorithm that meets your needs.

If you're looking for a strong leader who can manage teams and drive sales, most of the candidates produced by algorithmic hiring systems will be white males. This is because white males have historically held these types of positions and therefore the algorithms have learned to prioritize that history above any goals of having a diverse workforce. Sad, but true—and super important to know when you're looking through the results of the search you've paid a machine or a person to perform. This can be frustrating because many hiring managers turn to online platforms to help cut down on bias, not knowing that these algorithms are informed by bias.

Over the summer of 2019, the U.S. government's Equal Employment Opportunity Commission found reasonable cause to conclude that employees who programmed the codes for Facebook advertisements had violated the civil rights protection by excluding women and older individuals from seeing their job advertisements. ProPublica, a nonprofit investigative journalism newsroom, has covered this issue extensively and comprehensively.[1] This case is groundbreaking in that it is the first time the government has gone after a social media platform for its targeted ads, which are its primary revenue generator and the focus of many complaints of discriminatory practices.

Bias in algorithmic output has been identified in medical diagnostic machines, judicial sentencing, programs evaluating public school teachers, who gets a mortgage, and even when it comes to drone kill lists. We have become dependent on imperfect technology.

The hope was that in allowing math to calculate fairness, computer programs would compute without bias. But it's a fallacy that artificial intelligence is a kind of tabula rasa, allowing us to eradicate our human shortcomings by favoring logic over emotions.

In fact, what's happened is the opposite. We've programmed machines with our biases. To make matters worse, while humans can differentiate between implicit and explicit bias, a machine simply follows a series of if/then commands.

A 2017 study, published in *Science*,[2] proved that implicit associations—including prejudices—are communicated through language. "We show empirically that natural language necessarily contains human biases, and the paradigm of training machine learning on language corpora means that AI will inevitably imbibe these biases as well," Arvind Narayanan, co-author of the study, wrote about its findings.

I wrote a story for the *Boston Globe* about this same issue in 2017[3]:

THE SCIENTISTS FOUND that words like "flower" are more closely associated with pleasantness than insect. Female words were more closely associated with the home and arts than with career, math, and science. Likewise, African American names were more frequently associated with unpleasant terms than pleasant terms when compared to European American names.

This becomes an issue when recruiting programs trained on language sets like this are used to select resumes for interviews. If the program associates African American names with unpleasant characteristics, its algorithmic training will be more likely to select European American named candidates. Likewise, if the job-recruiting AI is told to search for strong leaders, it will be less likely to select women, because their names are associated with homemaking and mothering.

The scientists took their findings a step farther and found a 90 percent correlation between how feminine or masculine the job title ranked in their word-embedding research and the actual number of men versus women employed in 50 different professions, according to U.S. Labor statistics. The biases expressed through language directly relates to the roles we play in our life.

"I really try to combat when people think that it's the AI that's prejudiced and they don't get that the AI is just an extension of our culture," said Joanna Bryson, a computer scientist at the University of Bath in the United Kingdom and Princeton University. "It's not that robots are evil. It's that the robots are just us."

THIS IS AN essential point to understand. If you're trying to eliminate inherent bias, meaning one that isn't conscious, from your hiring process, you cannot ask computers to pick your candidate pool. You have to look outside the preselected talent because that pool will be based upon the current workforce, not the inclusive future workforce you are striving for.

∨ *This is an essential point to understand. If you're*
∨ *trying to eliminate inherent bias, meaning one that*
∨ *isn't conscious, from your hiring process, you cannot*
∨ *ask computers to pick your candidate pool.*

Key Takeaways

When using algorithmic programs to hire, be actively looking for skewed results:

- Count the number of female versus male applicants. If the results are weighted in favor of one gender, repeat the search looking to equal the pool.
- Also, always remember there are well-qualified people in every race, sex, ethnicity, age bracket, etc. If your results don't demonstrate that fact, then it is safe to assume something is wrong with your search.

THREE

Bring in Your People as Soon as Possible

Emily Chang's Lesson in Hiring too Soon

Marc* had a background in finance, with recent start-up experience. Emily Chang immediately recognized his can-do attitude as an asset she would need in her new executive position. The two met over lunch, set up by a mutual friend, which gave Chang another vote of confidence about Marc as a potential hire. As they talked, he seemed curious about her goals and the challenges she would face in her new role. She was intrigued by him too and liked his advice.

Chang had been appointed the chief commercial officer of a major hotel group, which came with a number of responsibilities including marketing operations, loyalty programs, revenue management, business intelligence, insights, partnerships, digital, guest experience, and the voice and call center.

Her goal in her new role with this new company was to drive revenue and market share through functional goals like guest experience, owner relationships, loyalty contribution, and digital channel optimization. Each of those initiatives relied heavily on strategic innovation.

In the hospitality industry, revenue comes from distribution, so distribution strategy is often the key to success. Distribution in this industry includes many ways of getting people into your hotel rooms. Selling hotel rooms through an app, call center, or website is considered direct distribution, whereas sales generated through online travel agencies, wholesale packages for tour groups, business-to-business partnerships, event or even wedding planners are a more indirect distribution model that is nonetheless essential to filling hotel rooms with paying customers.

"How you strategically allot your room inventory, how you optimize your business mix, and how you diversify your channel distribution is critical," Chang explained. "I really wanted somebody to come in and drive change with me, and when I talked to Marc about distribution, he got as geeked out as I did about it."

Most people would have jumped at the opportunity to work on any one of the six brands and three loyalty programs under Chang's charge; working on the revenue strategies for those programs is considered "fun" because you're dealing with incentives and promotions, but for her this was also a stimulating intellectual challenge. She saw brand loyalty programs as the biggest vehicle for massively improving revenue. Marc understood Chang's vision and shared her excitement.

"And I just thought, my gosh, he totally gets it," she remembered thinking. "He's asking all the questions I'm asking. I wanted to bring him in sooner than later."

And she did.

But her new entrepreneurial hire almost immediately clashed with the old guard.

"It was like an organ transplant failure," Chang recalled.

As is true of most organizations, new employees, like Chang, are viewed skeptically. What do they know that others don't? What changes are they planning? Are they planning on changing my role? Eliminating my job? Fear is a killer of innovation and when new people with new ideas arrive on the scene sometimes it's too much for the old guard.

Balance is required when hiring senior-level innovators. On the one hand, you must find someone who can think outside the box and see beyond the confines of what has already been done within the industry. But it's just as important to find an original thinker who can also work within the existing structure and respect the culture of the corporation. As Chang soon learned, an innovator is useless if they can't play within the established order of things. A novel idea is dead on arrival if the person with the idea is viewed as an outsider. They need to be able to collaborate with others or else they will not have an impact.

"The drive for change is important," Chang explained. "But an entrepreneurial mindset and a scrappy approach must be balanced with respect for the corporate culture. New leaders benefit from pausing to understand history, paying respect to how we got where we are. Equally important to the 'what' is the 'how': collaboratively building a vision for the future lays a path for everyone to engage, because no one person can come in and drive massive change."

> ⌄ *Balance is required when hiring senior-level*
> ⌄ *innovators. On the one hand, you must find someone*
> ⌄ *who can think outside the box and see beyond the*
> ⌄ *confines of what has already been done within*
> ⌄ *the industry. But it's just as important to find an*
> ⌄ *original thinker who can also work within the existing*
> ⌄ *structure and respect the culture of the corporation.*

It became clear that no one wanted to work with Marc. Chang approached individual leaders, one at a time, in an attempt to learn if the relationships could be salvaged. Her due diligence positioned her as a thoughtful leader who was aware of the unrest and took the time to carefully listen to feedback.

Most large corporations have the unspoken mantra: *but this is how we've always done it*. While we all want to lead innovative change, we must be realistic about the systems we have in place, why they're there, and if we *actually* want to disrupt them in order to move the needle in other ways. In most cases, the answer is we don't know how to do both. We value knowing what's expected of us, the right way to file a memo, call a meeting, plan for a new initiative.

When someone doesn't follow that code, it's upsetting because we don't know if we missed something. Did the protocol change? Or does this disrupter have permission to change these tried-and-true ways of doing things? And if so, what will they change next? All of that questioning distracts us from the day-to-day functions we're expected to perform. The result ranges from annoyance to complete disruption of the core business functions required to operate.

Chang soon learned that it wasn't so much Marc's ideas as it was his approach. People didn't perceive that he cared about the company, nor did he seem concerned with who he upset in the process of trying to implement his ideas. This left people feeling disregarded and hurt. Chang had liked his take-charge approach, but now recognized it could also become his downfall. Marc was so laser-focused on his goals, he missed critical cues that could have helped him adjust his approach.

Chang now had different worries on her mind. This guy was *her* hire. He was supposed to be *her guy* and now she faced internal unrest on her team. Like a pro, she tried to mediate. She spoke with everyone involved and conducted a thorough review. In an effort to show her new colleagues she took their feedback seriously, she really listened, which wasn't easy.

"When I saw the visceral reaction amongst the existing team leaders, I engaged them all one-by-one." Their grim expressions and a palpable sense of contention worried her. "We were facing total organ rejection."

The feedback was "overwhelmingly consistent." He had to go. She took a day to think about the concerns expressed and brainstorm how she could salvage these relationships. He was a great thinker and she valued his ideas. The trouble was his cavalier attitude—there was a general feeling around the office that Marc thought everyone else was subpar, that he was somehow better or knew more than those who'd spent their whole careers at this company. Chang couldn't undo that impression.

Sitting in her favorite egg chair overlooking the Huángpǔ River, she knew what she needed to do. She wanted to help him leave with dignity. And, perhaps most importantly, she wanted him to learn from his mistakes so that he too could grow from the experience. If he could learn to tread a little more softly, he'd surely be an exceptional innovator in the future. Chang knew she needed to manage her own perceptions.

"I knew there were some in the organization who might want to see me fail from this experience." She could hear them saying: "See, *your person* didn't work out. You don't understand our business or our culture. Maybe you should go too."

While her instinct was to soften the blow by taking the blame, she knew that wouldn't serve her goal to help him grow, nor was it entirely true. "We sat down, and I shared how much I appreciated him, and felt he had the right intellectual and strategic approach to the job," Chang said. "I also directly shared the feedback from the team. I handed him a printed copy that consolidated the inputs, which spoke for itself . . . in volumes."

Years later, Chang remembers how painful it was to watch his face fall, his disappointment visible. "I'll always remember resisting the urge to reassure him: 'It's not you. It's them. They're just not ready for this degree of change.' But I swallowed my words. Because I knew it wasn't entirely true. The organization was indeed resisting the change and resisting him. But his approach had also played a role. And so had I. I knew I had brought him in too early, when I hadn't fully gotten a sense of the place, or best known how to set him up for success."

Chang's lesson: it can be an important strategy for new leaders to bring in their own teams, but that path can be fatally flawed if the culture isn't well known to them when those hiring decisions are made. When you haven't spent enough time in an organization and you don't fully understand or feel immersed in the culture, don't bring somebody in yet, because you're unable to gauge whether that person can thrive in that environment or not.

∨   *Chang's lesson: it can be an important strategy for*
∨   *new leaders to bring in their own teams, but that*
∨   *path can be fatally flawed if the culture isn't well*
∨   *known to them when those hiring decisions are made.*

Key Takeaways

Hiring and being hired are moments of transition in a person's life. It is usually best to tread lightly when starting a new job, even if you're the new hiring manager.

- Get to know your coworkers and the new organization's culture before bringing anyone onboard.
- Ask for feedback. Bring seasoned staffers in on your preferences and see if they agree. Listen carefully to what they like and don't like about your candidates. This should inform your decisions and give you an education in the qualifications they value. You do not need to do exactly what they suggest, but seeking their input will allow you to see their perspective and make the best hires.
- Start by hiring junior people who will have fewer responsibilities. This will inform your understanding of hires that thrive and those that won't work out. Starting lower on the food chain may save you the mistake of putting the wrong senior leader in a position that doesn't pan out and reflects poorly on you.

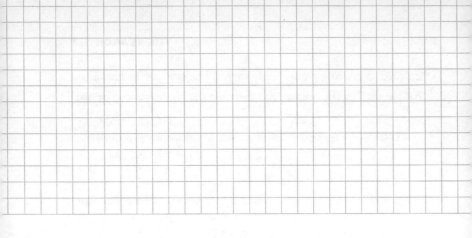

FOUR

Be Super Rigid about Roles

I t was a Friday afternoon in October and Sarah* didn't know if she could make it through one more interview. Two to go and she'd be on to her weekend. She desperately needed help in her toy store, but so far none of the applicants seemed up to the task. There was the guy who was more interested in playing with the display model train sets than working, and there was a teenage girl who sounded great but didn't have a license or a car and wasn't sure if her mom's schedule would allow for pick-ups and drop-offs *every* Saturday. The whole day had been a waste of interviews with people who would never work out. She looked at the clock and stood up from behind her desk, walked to her door, and waved to Steve, the next candidate, to come on in for his turn.

"Welcome, take a seat," she said. "Do you have any fun plans for the weekend?"

"Nope," he responded.

"Okay, so I see you worked at Emma's Candy shop last summer. How was that?"

"Fine," he mumbled.

"Just fine? You must love candy; did you get a sweet discount?" Sarah asked, throwing in a little pun in an attempt at lightening the mood. "I love their gummy worms; my daughter and I go there after soccer practice."

"Yeah, everyone likes the worms," Steve said, looking past Sarah out her window in a daze.

"So why did you decide to leave that position?"

"There were so many gross kids. They'd come in and stick their hands in the jars of candy and, you know, they'd cry and scream. It was annoying as hell."

"Oh, I can imagine," Sarah said, grateful for the candor, but confused if he thought this job would be much better.

"You know, we're a toy store. So, we have lots of kids come through here too. They don't stick their hands in sticky candy, though!" She needed a sales clerk, but probably not one who didn't want to be around children.

"Yeah, I know what you do. I just need a job or my mom says I have to leave, and I like living in the basement."

"Well, it's great to have an incentive and a place to live is definitely an incentive." Sarah was now actively thinking out loud. Could she really hire this guy? Maybe it would be like in a movie, he'd really take to the job and together they'd be a great team. Maybe? The holidays were weeks away and there was no way she could handle the store without an extra set of hands to help. Desperation was lowering her standards.

"What do you like about toys or working in a toy store? I think I need someone with a lot of positive energy, like Willy Wonka. I mean, not like this is a candy factory. I'm just looking for someone who has a childlike spirit. You know? I bought this place because I love playing with toys and thought there was a need for a toy store when the world feels saturated with screens. Do you like toys?"

"Yeah, sure," Steve said.

"Great!" Sarah hoped they'd turned a corner. "What's your favorite toy? Like from childhood or something maybe you still enjoy?"

"Oh, I love *Fortnite*. I play every night."

"Yeah, well, we don't sell video games." Sarah's resolve returned. She was not going to hire some video-game junkie to sell her beautiful wooden toys. That was not going to work. "I'm hoping to hire someone and get them trained and up to speed soon, before the holiday rush. I have a couple more people to talk to, so I'll be in touch," she said, standing to signal the end of the interview.

"Yeah, cool."

He was clearly not what she'd hoped for, but it was already November and she couldn't seem to find anyone who remotely resembled her dream candidate. The truth was, she was the dream candidate. When she was working the floor, she had great conversations with kids and parents and no one left empty-handed.

Sarah would learn what they liked or didn't like about certain games and found herself developing friendships with her customers, which certainly helped her generate repeat business. But it was impossible to run a small business and get it all done on her own. She needed help on the floor so she could place orders, manage the inventory, and handle all the upcoming promotions.

She made a few notes about Steve and welcomed the next candidate into her back office, which doubled as a stock room.

"Hi, I'm Jordan. My mom always comes in here and buys my little cousins stuff. She said you were hiring. I need a job. So, my mom said I should come by. So, I came by. And I was here on Wednesday and you said you'd interview me today, so now I'm here. Sorry, am I talking too much? People say I talk a lot. I just get nervous and then you know I want to fill the silence, my mom says it's nerves and that maybe when I'm older, like maybe when I'm in college, I'll get over it. But she says maybe it's because I don't have any confidence. You know? Like my friend Julie, she's got a lot of confidence; that's what everyone always says about her. I guess I don't really know what that means. Like she seems to be kind of bossy. Is that confident? Maybe I should try being more bossy, but how would that help me talk less? My mom says you can just *see* someone and know if they're confident? Like, you can see if their mouth is moving or if they're quiet? Are confident people usually quiet? How can they be bossy and quiet? Unless they have some magical telepathy, like they can control people without talking, but then I think they'd still be talking—just on the inside, like internally, right? Like, they'd be telling you what to do without saying it out loud. I wish I could do that, just keep my thoughts to myself. That kind of confuses me too, because people are always saying communication is the key to success, but then they say I talk too much. I guess I need to be more like Julie, only a quiet Julie who's not so bossy. Oh, I've probably just said too much. I'm doing it now, aren't I?"

Sarah, who had only just sat back down in her chair, now felt overwhelmed with doom listening to this applicant. How was she ever going to fill this position? The job market was so tight it felt like nearly half the online applicants she'd reached out to hadn't responded and then at least half of those that did were no-shows. The candidates who were coming in weren't right for the store floor. It was impossible to find anyone for this position.

"Hi, Jordan, maybe just take a deep breath. You certainly have a lot of energy and I like energy, so try to relax," Sarah said. The truth was, she did like a lot of energy, but she couldn't have her customers bombarded with the inner workings of a teenage girl the second they walked in the door, or worse still, when they were trying to pay for their purchase. They'd just throw the toys on the counter and run!

As Jordan took several yoga breaths in through her nose and out through her mouth, Sarah felt like she might cry. If the holidays came and went without any help on the floor, she might have to close the store. Sales were tight with all the competition online and from electronic games. The store had been her dream, but the hiring had been a nightmare.

"Why did you want to apply for a job with me?" Sarah asked.

"Oh, I just love it here," Jordan said, now visibly more calm. "You have so many great toys. I love how colorful it is and how happy you make people."

Wow! That was the best answer Sarah had heard from anyone. "Thank you. That's what I love too. Can you tell me a little bit about your work experience, Jordan?"

"Sure, so I've done a lot of babysitting. Kids are crazy and I love all that crazy! I am very good at keeping the house clean and I like to think parents are always happy when they come home and find the kitchen cleaner than when they left. I also really like to organize my closet and my mom's and sometimes my mom has me go to her friends' houses and they pay me to organize their closets and even, like, their kitchen pantries. I know I talk too much, but I don't rat on people, like I've found some weird things in my mom's best friend's closet, but you know I won't say anything, like I'm not going to tell you, even though I know you now want to know, and you're like wondering, what did Jordan find? But that's not my business—or yours—and when someone hires me for a job, I am happy they're paying me so I mind my business and work hard. I need money for college. You know I'm a junior and I really want to have fun at school next year and, like, not feel poor and stuff, so my mom says I should be saving now. Especially because I love to shop. I'm great at finding deals and replenishing. I love replenishing. I set up auto deliveries for all my mom's friends and help them with their household needs. I just go through their laundry supplies, their dishwasher soaps, you know, all that stuff, even kids' snacks, and have everything delivered monthly. It saves them time and I absolutely love it. I love shopping and organizing, and monthly services are the best of both worlds . . ."

"That all sounds good, but have you ever worked in a store or handled money or a cash register?" Sarah interrupted Jordan's rant.

"Oh no, my mom says I'm terrible with money. She always finds money in my pants pockets when she does the wash and she says she's never met anyone more irresponsible when it comes to keeping track of money. She once sent me to the grocery store with $40 and told me to buy a few things. I came home with like $5 and she was so mad. I had somehow lost like $12. I still don't know how I did that. She says I wasn't paying attention when I got change. But I didn't bring a calculator. How was I supposed to know how much change to get from them? Feels a little unfair. But, no, I've never worked in a store, and I think my mom would say I shouldn't be trusted with money."

"Well, that's going to be hard in this position, because you'd be ringing customers up."

"Oh no, seriously?" Now Jordan looked like she was going to cry.

"I think I need to talk to a couple of other people and then make a decision about this role. I really appreciate you coming in," Sarah said, ending this interview.

It was a dilemma. She needed help in the store, but none of the candidates were quite right. Steve seemed way too low energy. Sarah could imagine him just sitting behind the counter and playing with his phone. And Jordan was too high energy; she would talk customers right out of the store.

She made a list of all the job functions she needed help with. It was clear to her that she'd have to pick the best out of this limited, not-so-great pool. But as she reviewed her list, she had an idea. It was obvious that she was the right candidate for the front of the store. She really couldn't have Steve working with the kids and their parents. But what if she trained Jordan to manage the back of the store? She could come in for a couple hours a few days a week after school and she could certainly get the stockroom organized on Saturdays. Maybe she'd like the ordering—it was a lot like shopping and the monthly deliveries she loved arranging. And maybe Jordan would be the perfect organizer. She wouldn't have to deal with money, and she could help with in-store events when needed. This was the best solution. It allowed Sarah to do what she loved and still get all the back-end work done.

Sometimes the key to a bad talent pool is reexamining your needs and abilities so you can see how to make them all work together. Recalibrating the roles allowed Sarah to fill her hiring needs and put the right people in the right places without having to worry that any necessary function would suffer.

Sure enough, Sarah and Jordan made a great team. The store had its best Christmas sales ever. Sarah greeted and played with each customer, while Jordan organized wonderful displays and refilled orders with such competency that she soon gained a whole new sense of self-confidence.

Key Takeaways

Remember there are always many more moving pieces when it comes to hiring than we tend to acknowledge.

- If someone is great for a role that is different than what you were searching for, consider shuffling people around to get each peg in the right hole.
- There are always people who can be flexible and then those that can only do (or only want to do) a finite list of tasks. If you can be flexible, you will find you have many more opportunities to hire people for those specific functions.
- In a small business, creatively thinking about roles and allowing for creative solutions will win every day.

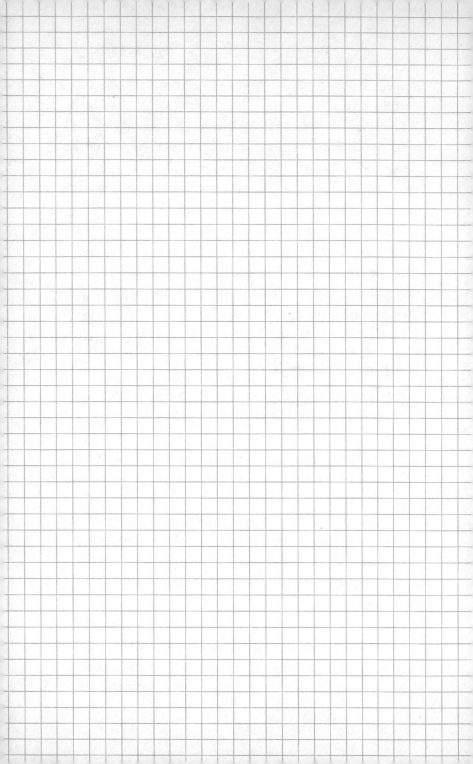

2 Section

The Interview

You've conducted your search and now you have a list of candidates you need to choose between. This next section will explore the different ways to evaluate a job applicant in person.

To use the dating analogy again, remember, a first date is usually not an honest representation of who you are, and the same is true for the first interview. The candidate will naturally be a bit nervous and will be conscientiously trying to to present themselves in the best possible way.

The web is filled with advice about being "professional," preparing properly, and asking good questions. While this may be helpful to the applicant, it can make the interviewer's job harder. You need to cut through the facade and figure out who you're dealing with.

Are they going to work hard, does their experience fit the needs of the role, and what are some characteristics they have that set them apart from the rest of the pool?

The best way to determine if someone is right for the gig is to interview them. Ideally you would talk to the person a couple times and have other people in your organization talk with the candidate too. Companies invest a lot in their employees and every new hire should be viewed as a new opportunity to further the mission.

This section will consider mistakes people make in the interview stage of hiring so you can avoid those same errors.

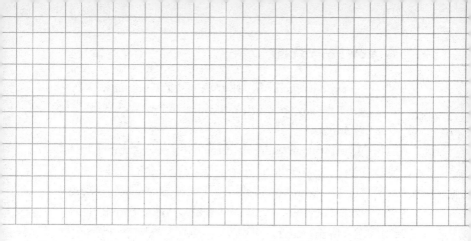

FIVE

Start the Interview with the Wrong Questions

Your time is limited, and you already have a picture of the candidate from what is listed on his or her resume and cover letter. You may even have information from other people's notes from previous interviews with this candidate. But that doesn't mean you should start the interview with big, potentially loaded questions.

Here are some examples of the wrong questions to start with, unless you're hoping to make the candidate nervous and stiff:

- You've had four jobs in five years. Why don't you stay anywhere longer?

- I see you worked with The Weinstein Company. Did you have any uncomfortable interactions with Mr. Weinstein?
- When you left your job at the bank in September, it looks like you didn't start at your next job until January. Were you looking for work that whole time?
- Your dad referred you. Is that how you've gotten your jobs in the past?

Those may all feel uncomfortable and you are probably sophisticated enough to know not to ask those kinds of questions. But you might ask these:

- Why do you think you're the right fit for this job?
- Why are you looking to leave your current position?
- If you could change one thing about your current position, what would it be?

Those feel more appropriate, but the timing would be off if you started with them. They are called open-ended questions because they open the conversation to a wide array of possible answers. Starting any conversation with open-ended questions that are loaded with pressure for at least one party establishes a power dynamic that will likely lead to a more reserved interaction. If your goal is to connect with the interviewee, then you want to save the open-ended questions for a point in the interview when things are more comfortable than they are at the onset. Remember, the candidate wants the job, and is very self-aware and likely anxious. Your job as the interviewer is to make the candidate feel comfortable so you can get an accurate—rather than formulaic—read on the candidate as a person, beyond his or her resume.

When interviewing sources and job applicants, I've learned that starting with closed-ended questions gives the person a chance to settle into the interview. Even saying, "Let's start with some basics," gives the candidate a chance to get to know you, to look around your office, to settle in. The beginning of the interview isn't the time to extract new information, it's your opportunity to develop a rapport with the candidate and allow them to feel more comfortable so they can articulate complex answers more honestly later on. Asking simple questions allows the interviewee to feel more in control. When they supply an answer to a closed-ended question, they feel like they're doing well and they start to like you as an interviewer, because the experience is not painful, it is not too hard, and they can score their own answers. The beginning of the interview is like a pass-fail test, and almost all candidates will pass. That builds confidence in the process and allows you both to move on to more nuanced questions, where you'll learn who this candidate really is.

> ∨ *When interviewing sources and job applicants,*
> ∨ *I've learned that starting with closed-ended questions*
> ∨ *gives the person a chance to settle into the interview.*

Closed-ended questions are questions with clear answers. What's your name? Where did you go to school? Who was your last employer? There is no need for analysis or interpretation. Having these answers at hand puts the candidate at ease, allowing you to move into the open-ended questions, which do not have "right or wrong" answers.

- What were your favorite parts about the jobs you've previously had?
- What do you hope to learn from our company?
- Why did you apply for this position?
- What do you know about what we do here?
- Do you have a five-year plan?
- When you started at your current company, what was that like?
    - How has your role changed since?
    - When you look at your day-to-day responsibilities, what do you wish you could change about your role?

Once you've made that initial connection, you can ask more probing questions without derailing the conversation. And you should ask questions that pinpoint the source of your candidate's motivation and drive. You want to know if they'll deliver results for your company, but you also want to know that they'll be happy in the role. Learning what they didn't like about their previous job is a great way to discern whether or not they'll thrive in a new position.

You can keep going with open-ended questions all day long, but you can't unhear answers so ask carefully. For example, a question about a five-year plan could lead to an uncomfortable answer: "Well, I hope to meet someone and have kids in the next five years." Suddenly, the interview becomes tricky. If you don't offer the job to that candidate, you might be faced with questions about discrimination. You can't ask people what their personal plans are. Try phrasing the question in a different way: "Sticking strictly to your professional goals, what's your five-year plan?" This sets the clear expectation that you are not asking and in fact do not want to hear anything about the candidate's personal life.

The art of the interview is also about making people feel comfortable. So, try sharing some of your own stories. This creates a more connected interview format and you're more likely to hear who this candidate really is and what drives her.

You can share stories about what your company was like when you started there or what you think separates it from its competitors. You can talk about the culture—about whether or not people are social, or how the boss sits in the middle of the room to encourage a collaborative environment (or, conversely, about how the boss sits in a corner office and expects everyone to stay on top of their own workloads in a very independent environment). The more honest you are, the more the person you're interviewing will be open about their experiences, letting you know what excites them most about the opportunity or whether they have reservations about your company.

Finding the right candidate isn't always about convincing someone your workplace is perfect for them; it's really about getting to know them and figuring out if they'd be a good fit for your specific office in a specific role. It is your job to get them talking about why they want the position and to set clear expectations about what will be required of them. That sounds simple, but it can be overwhelming.

> ∨ *The more honest you are, the more the person*
> ∨ *you're interviewing will be open about their*
> ∨ *experiences, letting you know what excites them*
> ∨ *most about the opportunity or whether they have*
> ∨ *reservations about your company.*

Try to take notes while the person is talking and try not to use a computer. You will find that when you're writing on a pad of paper, there will be moments of silence. These are often the times when the candidate will speak up. They'll ask an important question or tell a story you might not have been able to draw out with a direct question. No one really enjoys silence in an interview, it's awkward, but if you have patience you will find the other person fills the void for you.

SIX

Make the Candidate Defensive

If we take the dating analogy and extend it to the interview process, it's easy to see how you can quickly screw things up. The hiring process is left to deducing two things: Can this candidate do the job, and do you think this candidate will work well within the culture and community of the company?

Any good reporter will tell you that the best way to turn an interview into a hostile conversation is to start by asking emotional questions; you haven't developed any kind of rapport with the subject and they will immediately feel put on the defensive. Opening with complex emotional questions is a deal killer. For example: "I see you were referred by your father, who's a senior partner here; is that how you've gotten jobs in the past?" Or "It looks like you were in a fraternity. Does that mean you're a big drinker?"

Okay, so you're not that dumb, you wouldn't ask those kinds of questions. But you might say something like: "I see you live in Williamsburg. I used to live there, do you like it?"

You might think that's an icebreaker, that it's a way to connect and relate to each other. But, you're now asking a personal question and you don't know what this might bring up and out. Maybe your candidate hates the neighborhood because it's become a hipster mecca (or maybe they moved there *because* it's a hipster mecca). Either way, it unintentionally invites judgment into the conversation.

"Tell me about your perfect day when you're not working." This sounds perfectly harmless until the candidate answers that their idea of a perfect day is lying on the couch recovering from a night of partying, that they like to sit around and watch TV all day. In fact, that's their favorite thing to do. While that may be the most honest answer you get all day, it will be a hard thing to forget when it's time to evaluate how they'll fit in at a company filled with people who wake up early to get a five-mile run in before work. Or maybe you're a recovering alcoholic, and the candidate's celebration of drinking culture rubs you the wrong way. You now have strong personal feelings about this candidate that may consciously or unconsciously interfere with your ability to judge them objectively as an applicant. The easiest way to avoid this conundrum is to do just that: avoid it. Don't ask questions you don't want to know the answers to.

> ⌄ *The easiest way to avoid this conundrum is to do just*
> ⌄ *that: avoid it. Don't ask questions you don't want to*
> ⌄ *know the answers to.*

SEVEN

Questions to Ask
If You Want to Be Sued

- How old are you?
- Do you date men or women?
- Where's your church?
- Where were your parents born?
- When do you expect to get pregnant?
- Do you have any disabilities that will hurt your job performance?
- What do you do with your kids while you're at work?
- How often are you sick?
- What kinds of medical problems have you had in the last five years?

- Do you see a psychiatrist?
- Would you like to have dinner with me sometime?
- Are you married?
- How much money does your husband make?

EIGHT

Ruin the Interview by Doing All the Talking

Another way to ruin an interview, and most employers and human resource reps have had to learn this the hard way, is to fill empty space with your own voice: you want to share, not dominate. All too often when we feel nervous, we talk a lot. Then the candidate leaves, and you feel exhausted, suddenly realizing you didn't learn a thing about the person you were supposed to be interviewing. That's a lost opportunity. One of my favorite compliments I have ever received was from a source I had spent hundreds of hours with as a reporter. He told me, "I feel I could go to dinner with you and leave having bared my soul and yet still not know any more about you than I did when we sat down." This source was comfortable with me and shared things he hadn't told his wife. I don't think I had any specific trick in mind to make him share so openly, but I was intensely curious about his life, his experiences, and how he made decisions, sometimes in very dangerous situations. Because I'd read about his conviction, his trial, and had talked to many members of his family, I knew him from many perspectives, all of which informed how I approached him.

As a journalist at ABC News's *20/20* and *Primetime*, I often found myself dropped into a crisis where I had to build a relationship with many people—victims, families, lawyers, local media, and so forth. I tried to learn about the culture before I dropped in and I always tried to empathize and think of how to show my respect to the people involved. It is essential to know as much as you can about a person before you interview them, but the very best way to develop a rapport with someone is to be genuinely curious about them. I find people to be wonderfully fascinating. I have never interviewed anyone I found to be boring.

This is likely because I had an honest interest in learning about them. This is a very different take than a lawyer might have. Lawyers ask questions as a way of getting to some specific point or fact. They also use their power—expressed through their ability to demand answers to questions—to intimidate and cause a stress response in people under oath. This is very different from a journalist or an employer interviewing someone.

When you've researched someone and know a bit about them before the interview starts, or you have notes from a previous round of interviews, you can quickly get into the "what was it like when" type questions that go to the candidate's drive or interests in a more intimate way.

When you start the interview with the closed-ended questions, you're essentially confirming data you already know or filling in gaps you may have in your knowledge of their factual past. When you switch to open-ended questions, you are getting more into the essence of the person. There is no specific right or wrong answer to open-ended questions.

In my work as a business owner—I run three women's health and weight loss centers, called Prime Fitness & Nutrition—I tell my managers who work with our members to do the same things I would do as a reporter. They should be able to fill out three pages of information on every member, front and back sides, that includes their health goals, their personal goals, points of stress in their lives, and why our women's health-focused programming can help them.

Yet, if I went to any of the members and asked them to fill out one page on any of the staff, they wouldn't be able to do it, and that would surprise them. The relationship is always focused on the member, client, source, or potential hire. This information is the key to interacting with them. When you're hiring, you want to get a sense of the interviewee's character, which means you need to be careful with your questions to remove inherent bias, and you must learn to listen carefully. If you talk a lot about you, the company, the role, you may find the candidate has learned more about you than you have about them. The best way to avoid the over-talking pitfall is to have a connected conversation. You want to get to know the person as a human, not just an employee, in order to have a sense of whether they will work well in your business.

Even in those moments of awkward silence, try to be quiet. Wait for the candidate to fill the space. You may be surprised by what they share. Often the things we use to fill space are stories we might not have thought to share if we were asked. They are the unprepared remarks that reveal a lot about who we are and how we think.

> ✓ *When you're hiring, you want to get a sense of the*
> ✓ *interviewee's character, which means you need to be*
> ✓ *careful with your questions to remove inherent bias,*
> ✓ *and you must learn to listen carefully. If you talk a lot*
> ✓ *about you, the company, the role, you may find the*
> ✓ *candidate has learned more about you than you*
> ✓ *have about them.*

Listening can be harder than talking:

Ask a question, wait for the answer, and then repeat the answer back in your own language.

Interviewer: How did you like working for Harley?

Interviewee: Oh, she's amazing. She has so much energy and is such a creative thinker, I loved working for her. I learned a lot from her.

Interviewer: Sounds like you liked working for Harley. So, you thought she was creative and you learned a lot. Tell me more about what you learned from her.

Interviewee: Well, one example would be her approach to problems with our supply chain; often the deadlines weren't met. Harley came up with the idea of always sourcing from two vendors, then incentivizing them to get the delivery done or they wouldn't get the order. This created a competition through the first stages of production and basically remedied our delivery problems. She did tons of stuff like that.

SEE HOW THE interviewer was able to get a much more specific and interesting answer from the candidate by simply acknowledging that she was listening carefully? The interviewer talked but said nothing new. Her ability to paraphrase back what the interviewee said furthered the discussion in a meaningful way.

NINE

Terrible Questions versus Great Open-Ended Questions

Since the interview is your best chance to mess things up with a potential hire, we're going to spend a little more time on the ways you should and shouldn't handle questions. How the conversation goes sets the tone for the whole relationship and how the prospect feels about you and your business. You need to get this right.

Here are questions that hopefully lend themselves to a better conversation revealing more about the candidate than just the applicant's well-prepared answers.

Who was your favorite boss ever? What did you learn about yourself while you were in that role?

When you were in college, did you take any classes that you really enjoyed outside of your major? What was it about that class that you liked so much? (This will bring out something special that you might not find out otherwise.)

Ask the applicant about a class taken outside of their major in college that has stayed with them, or that they really enjoyed. This will tell you something about them that will reveal a bit more about their personality, the way they think and learn. For example: maybe the candidate liked a History of Science class because it put the experiments in the lab into the context of how these discoveries were first devised, and that made the lab work more fulfilling. Or perhaps a candidate loved his studio art class because it helped him organize his thoughts in a visual way, which he realized helped him form the arguments he made in a government class and ultimately led to his winning the big debate that year.

We all have a variety of interests. When you ask someone in a job interview what they're interested in, they will feel pressure to tell you something that fits with the job they're applying for, but when you ask them specifically about something that's not related to an area they're supposed to have mastered, then you will open a gateway to what makes them tick.

You'll see this with athletes too. Ask anyone applying for a business job who also played a sport in college why they enjoyed *that* sport and you'll hear great stories about their ability to perform under pressure, their competitive spirit, and likely how they respond to failure. You'll learn whether they were coachable and whether they thrive from positive or negative feedback.

All of these things offer insight into qualities that may make them a more preferable candidate. But you won't hear about these kinds of differentiating qualities by asking these applicants what they liked about college.

Often the activities that are considered outside of our core competencies are the ones that show our character and values in a more authentic way. People will be well prepared to answer questions about their previous jobs, classes, etc., but they are not as likely to have prepped answers about their charity work, their love of tennis, or their favorite trips. These stories will give you a sense of the person. Looking at the outside activities listed on an applicant's resume allows the interviewer to find a more personal avenue into the conversation.

> ∨ *Often the activities that are considered outside of*
> ∨ *our core competencies are the ones that show our*
> ∨ *character and values in a more authentic way. People*
> ∨ *will be well prepared to answer questions about their*
> ∨ *previous jobs, classes, etc., but they are not as likely*
> ∨ *to have prepped answers about their charity work,*
> ∨ *their love of tennis, or their favorite trips. These*
> ∨ *stories will give you a sense of the person.*

Key Takeaways

Finding a way into someone's personality and motivations is hard but can be important.

- Be friendly and ask questions that might be tangential to the person's background.
- Think of things people around the office like to do when they're not at work and tell the candidate, then ask them about something on their resume that might be more of a leisure activity, but try to stick to the resume or something they've already told you.
- You can always use yourself as an example: "When I'm not here I love taking my kids on hikes. We've been doing it for years and it's such a nice way for us to come together as a family. One of the things I appreciate about this company is that we're given passes to local museums, nature preserves, and I often bump into coworkers on weekends out enjoying those perks. Did your previous employer offer anything like that that you may miss?

TEN

Don't Make a Connection
Doug Stone's Lesson from Academia[1]

The goal of any interview is to learn more about the candidate than what's listed on their resume. Sure, you need to be respectful and, of course, follow the laws of your state regarding appropriate questions, but you also need to find a way to connect with the person applying for the job. If you're not striving for that goal, you might as well just hire off the resume. The point of the interview is to connect and learn a little more about the person's motivations, interests, and, of course, his or her character. You have to ask questions and create an environment that allows your candidate to open up. In this chapter, we're going to hear how one expert interviewer and listener tried to connect with an applicant, but struggled until the very end of the process, when their breakthrough made all the difference.

Candidates, much like reporters' sources, are sometimes nervous. Many have been coached on how to present themselves and their ideas. They may not open up easily. Doug Stone, who is a managing partner at Triad Consulting Group and a lecturer on law at Harvard Law School, where he teaches negotiation, says he once made a big mistake and almost missed out on hiring a terrific applicant because he struggled to connect with her.

Anyone who makes it to an interview with Stone is highly qualified, so the interviews are an essential step in deciphering the good from the great. In order to be an excellent negotiation teacher, one must be personable, emotionally intelligent, and able to connect with others—essentially, they must embody the skills they will be teaching.

In any highly competitive field, the interview is a chance to better understand how someone thinks and how that thinking will aid in the work, the culture, and the learning that happens in the office.

At first, Stone found this particular candidate's answers to be reserved. Stone knows job interviews are about finding an emotional or intellectual connection with the interviewee, so he tried to make the candidate comfortable, tried to use humor, tried everything he could think of, but her answers were stiff and despite his best efforts he couldn't get a sense of who she really was beyond the great resume.

Harvard Law School's Program on Negotiation is internationally recognized as a collaborative environment. It is ground zero for mutually beneficial negotiation training. Colleagues workshop, strategize, role-play, and try out new approaches to conflict resolution all day, every day. A person with a scripted approach to life wouldn't fit in well. And it was important for

Stone to know that any new hire could jump in and contribute, speak up when they disagreed with someone else's idea, and help move the overall mission forward.

One of the key principles in the negotiation training centers on the idea that when we form friendships, find commonalities, and really learn to listen to each other, we can come to agreements that benefit both parties without either side feeling compromised. If the candidate couldn't find a way to relate to Stone in the interview, how would she teach students to connect in even more stressful situations? He thought this candidate probably wasn't the right fit for the teaching position he was filling.

"And then at the end of the interview, she started talking about her five-year-old daughter and how she had just dropped her off at school for the first time in kindergarten," Stone said. "And then she started tearing up a little bit."

That opening led Stone and the applicant into a much more revealing conversation. "We just started talking and she was saying, 'You're raising somebody, and they've never really been out in the world, and what a big day it is for that person and how scary it is for them.' We just started talking about that and I thought, well, this is exactly the kind of person that I want to work with."

When he saw the candidate's ability to empathize, he could start to see how she approaches challenging situations. Stone was looking for someone to teach negotiation, which is deeply rooted in understanding people and how they think, feel, and act, and when she talked about her daughter, she displayed all the traits of a great negotiation teacher: she was able to deeply empathize, examine risks, rewards, and so forth.

"The advice is just make a connection, somehow," he said. "Up to that point, in that particular interview, she was doing the other thing [people think they need to do], which is trying to be *super* professional, which to me is distancing and makes me feel like I can't really tell anything about this person. I'm not learning about this *person*. And then when she started sharing about her daughter, she was really sharing about her values and how she saw the world and what was important to her. And I shared those values. So that was good."

Key Takeaways

Even if you're not one of the country's best negotiators, you still want to connect with the person you're hiring.

- Find a way to make a connection.
- Empathy is a powerful way to connect.
- Consider sharing your own story and see if you feel a sense of empathy from the candidate and perhaps they will share a meaningful story with you as well.

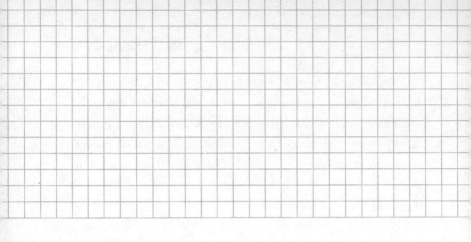

ELEVEN

Only Look at Her Resume

Doug Levine's Lessons from
Government Hiring[1]

Everyone wanted a position on the governor's team. And, in the rare moments when they had an opening, a whooshing sound could be heard from Fenway to the North End, as a vacuum of talent flooded their job board. When Doug Levine listed a position for a new lawyer in his Executive Office of Public Safety, a cabinet-level agency within the governor's office, he was overwhelmed with resumes.

Private sector attorneys looking to escape corporate law for public service impact polished up their CVs, and fresh meat from Boston College to Harvard jockeyed for positions. The range of applicants was always incredible, and perhaps the toughest job fell to the few who had to select the right lawyer from this elite talent pool.

Their office was small, the lawyers worked closely together, and that meant the new hire would have to be amiable, brilliant, humble, and hardworking. Extracting those characteristics from a resume and a couple of interviews was no small task.

Doug Levine was one of the people tasked with hiring the new lawyer. He'd started as general counsel for the Executive Office of Public Safety and Security under Governor Deval Patrick and continued on as special counsel when Charlie Baker was elected. There they worked on important decisions that impacted the state, so the jobs were important and coveted.

"You can go with academic prowess and experience, and we had both," Levine said of those who applied for the position. "We had people who had incredible academic credentials. We had people who had years and years of experience, and it was kind of a balancing act too because we had people that just had too much experience. They'd been practicing law for twenty-plus years. We had a lot of people apply who wanted to make a shift from the private sector into government. And this was our lower- or entry-level attorney position."

He knew that the lower-level position came with a lot of grunt work—work a senior partner at a top private firm hadn't done for decades, like responding to very basic public records requests or tracking down a specific statute or case. Expecting someone with such a distinguished resume to do this kind of remedial work might be uncomfortable, even if the candidate appreciated the impact the rest of the team was having.

These factors all needed to be considered, because the real goal was to have a team that gelled and could have the maximum output. And the last thing anyone wanted was to have such a great talent pool and somehow select the wrong candidate who, in six months, would be missing their big salary and massive support staff and decide to quit this public service position. This was a job for a lawyer who understood that they'd need to roll up their sleeves and pitch in and help wherever they were needed, even if that meant making copies for a meeting.

Working for the government was different than the private sector in many ways. When the government jobs were filled with earnest younger grads, they often did a good job for a few years. Their optimism and Ivy League degrees allowed them to contribute in a meaningful way, but very often they would start to see their former classmates making three to five times what they made working for the Commonwealth and that would wear on them. It can be hard to remain dedicated to the low-wage work of government when you see your former classmates living in mansions in Boston's exclusive Back Bay, paid for by corporate deals and contested divorces.

You went to law school because you were going to change the world, to protect the unprotected, and ensure that government led by example. But the truth is, that manifesto often has an expiration date. When life gets expensive, and you know you can earn more in the private sector, it is damn hard to stay and fight the good fight.

The cost of living in Boston is always one of the highest in the nation, so you might find that while your job is defending the reputation and practices of this great city, you personally cannot afford to live in it. Your sense of purpose naturally shifts from one of large-scale impact to direct family–level impact. In the long run, the private sector's impressive pay scale too often wins out. No matter how determined someone was in law school to contribute to a political campaign or advance an initiative to end homelessness, when the mortgage payment is due or the priorities of your family demand more income, those virtuous ideals take a back seat. Levine understood all of this and had to weigh these factors when he considered the wide range of applicants from the young grads fresh out of law school to the older candidates looking to pivot. Both sets had benefits and risks associated with them.

An inverse problem presented itself with the private sector folks who grew bored with the legal affairs of the rich. Their drive to help make the world a better place was palpable and there were few people who found that loads of money actually made them happier if they were not also making an impact. This is why many firms allow their associates and partners to do pro bono work. But pro bono work can be like a gateway drug for lawyers: the sweet taste of making a difference. Making policy directly impacting survivors of sexual assault versus managing the affairs of an old, rich dude and his spoiled offspring bring very different feelings of satisfaction. So, it's no surprise many lawyers in town wanted an interview with Levine when he posted the opening for a lawyer in their impactful office.

"We're a small office; the whole Executive Office of Public Safety isn't more than twenty or twenty-five people, and we were four lawyers," Levine explained. "So, I think that trying to find that fit was challenging. We ended up with somebody who had interned [for them] and who had a really good sense [of the work and expectations] and obviously had made the connections and the relationships with our office and with the twelve agencies that we directly oversee, as well as the governor's office too."

And Levine's decision to hire from within is typical. Trying someone out without the obligation of a longer-term commitment can be ideal. Many big law firms invite summer interns to social events. This isn't because they're nice or especially inclusive of the junior staffers, it's to see what they're "really like." Going to a party with your boss is a chance for you to get to know each other. If you're the guy who is usually hanging from the chandelier, you should know that most social events organized by the employers are informal character tests.

In case you were wondering, you still need to behave like you were in the office, even if there's an open bar. Any junior human resource rep knows the integrity of a person can be hard to evaluate in the formal process where there are legal limits to what can be asked in an interview. But the summer party, well that's a free-for-all. Companies, law firms, government agencies—they need to trust that their new hires will represent them well. Because when they don't, their bad behavior can tarnish the whole brand.

When someone is arrested, the headline usually includes identifiers, like where they work. A few hypothetical examples: The president's attorney was arrested for drunk driving. Boston Children's hospital doctor killed his wife. *Boston Globe* reporter found naked in Quincy Market.

Even if the crime didn't happen at work, the offense will always be linked back to the offender's profession and, if their position is noteworthy, the name of the employer. Knowing how your employees behave off-hours is important to employers, but it's not always easy information to obtain. That's why parties can serve an important function.

Summer interns were an important part of Levine's working group at the Executive Office for Public Safety. They hired law students to come work for the summer, and it was often hard to know what they'd get from the intern until they actually started.

- ∨ *Knowing how your employees behave off-hours is*
- ∨ *important to employers, but it's not always easy*
- ∨ *information to obtain. That's why parties can serve*
- ∨ *an important function.*

"You can only gather so much information about a person's personality and work ethic from their CV, unless you can really find your way in during a phone call with their references," Levine said. Levine previously served as a federal government lawyer working for both the Department of Justice and the Department of Homeland Security.

"When they do a background check for people who are getting federal security clearances, you give them a list of references, but then they get other names from your references so they can talk to those folks to try to really get a fuller picture. We don't do that when we're hiring. We just call the references. And so, the references, they're usually glowing, or they wouldn't be the candidate's references."

And hiring that way can result in some bad decisions.

"This one person that I'm thinking of A) had a terrible work ethic and B) a *really* bad attitude," Levine said of a summer hire who turned out to be a dud despite a great resume and positive references. "They'd just give you yes or no answers. Not a thoughtful person at all. No interest in really being there. Almost like 'I have to do an internship this summer to put on my resume, so when I go back to law school, I've done X for the summer and I worked for the Baker administration.'"

Levine says that was his worst hire and it really bothered him that the intern had snatched up a competitive position from someone else, someone who would have probably worked harder and contributed more. He said when they evaluated that candidate it was his credentials, his strong ranking, that pushed him to the top of the pile. That was the mistake. Levine says you have to evaluate someone on much more than just their resume.

Next time, Levine knew better. By nature, Levine is a funny person. His charm naturally draws people to him. He's a town selectman in his small community outside of Boston and a natural leader who rallies others to the cause, whether it be at the state capitol or at one of his daughter's friends' birthday parties. It should come as no surprise that an interview with Levine would probably leave you feeling pretty disarmed and comfortable. He'd likely start with some easy questions to warm you up. But you'd be mistaken if you assumed his warm smile trumped his critical eye. He is smart, wicked smart, and his Harvard degree is proof that while he's laughing and cracking jokes, he's also evaluating your character, your work ethic, and your credentials; he's just doing it in the nicest way possible.

Because Levine prioritizes credentials and social intelligence equally, he uses both the interview and the candidate's references to get a more complete picture. And what he's learned is that informal personal references are always the best way to really know someone. Calling up an old professor whom the candidate mentioned they'd taken a class with, whom you also took a class with, is a great way to get a read on a job applicant. Same goes for applicants who have worked in other departments or with other people you have a relationship with—you need to do whatever you can to properly evaluate the person applying for the job while operating within the confines of your state's laws. Levine says having several rounds of interviews and having different people in your office talk with candidates is another way to boil down to who the person really is and how he will perform on the job.

⌄ *Because Levine prioritizes credentials and social*
⌄ *intelligence equally, he uses both the interview and*
⌄ *the candidate's references to get a more complete*
⌄ *picture. And what he's learned is that informal*
⌄ *personal references are always the best way to*
⌄ *really know someone.*

"Over the course of twenty years, since graduating from law school, I would say one thing to be aware of is that I find that you can't necessarily pair somebody's academic credentials with social intelligence. In the professional context it's great when somebody is book smart and they're able to make connections in their mind quickly and be able to explain complex information and digest it quickly," Levine said. "But it doesn't necessarily mean they have the social intelligence and that's what you're supposed to be able to suss out in an interview, which is a tall order when you're only meeting somebody a single time. So, I guess multiple rounds of interviews in that sense are good because then they're having to connect with other people in your office and then the other staff are going to be able to weigh in on the candidate's social skills as well. But for me the social intelligence factor is a key and it's not easy to ascertain that from a resume. You want to know that *I want to be in this person's space for most of my waking life every day.*"

∨ *I guess multiple rounds of interviews in that sense*
∨ *are good because then they're having to connect*
∨ *with other people in your office and then the other*
∨ *staff are going to be able to weigh in on the*
∨ *candidate's social skills as well. But for me the social*
∨ *intelligence factor is a key and it's not easy to*
∨ *ascertain that from a resume.*

Key Takeaways

More than meets the eye: when trying to get to know a candidate, you must remember that different methods will deliver different results. Here are some examples of avenues to learn about the job applicant:

- Resume
- Group interview
- One-on-one interviews
- Informal gatherings
- Referrals
- Unofficial referrals
- Internships
- Hiring someone as a consultant

3

The Hire

Y ou've done all the work! The original pile of resumes has been sorted and filed. Candidates were called, interviews scheduled, and a decision was made. Your work is done, right? Wrong!

You may have found the candidate you want, but you need to be sure they are the right person for the job and that they are ready to get to work. This next stage of the hiring process is often overlooked. The start of any relationship is the time to set clear expectations. This is the time to show the employee you respect them, you think they'd be a great fit, and you're excited to welcome them aboard.

The offer stage is also the opportunity to hear from the potential employee in a more honest and open way. Once the offer has been made, the tables turn and the candidate has the chance to ask the questions. You want them to say yes to the offer, but don't let that eagerness trump the need to be honest about the culture, the expectations, the duties, or anything else you fear might turn them away. It is always better to have the candidate decide it's not the right job before they start than it is to fudge the truth hoping they'll take the opportunity and then find they're unhappy, or worse, have them quit shortly into the position.

Before you make the offer, make sure it's the offer you want to make and one that is being made for the right reasons. Then you can approach the offer in an open and honest way.

This final section of the book will look at how the final stage of the hiring process has to take into account many variables. You can easily mess this up. This section will go into detail on how the wrong candidate sometimes gets the offer, how the environment can drastically shift your hiring needs, and how making the right, or wrong, offer will impact the future of the organization.

TWELVE

Hire Someone You Want to Be Friends with, Even If They're Not the Most Qualified[1]

Jason* had worked in reality TV for decades. He was one of the masterminds behind the hit series *Golden Ages*, which showcased the dramatic lives of wealthy women in retirement communities. That show made him a leading producer in Hollywood, but his next project would be what defined him. Sure, he'd made *Golden Ages* a huge success, but could he do it again? There was a lot of pressure on him to succeed, not the least of which was coming from him.

After looking around at the opportunities in Los Angeles, Jason decided it was too stifling to be creative in the city that knew him as the old lady producer. He needed a change of scenery if he was going to hit it big again. He couldn't be constantly reminded of his past while he was trying to design his future.

He had heard there was a revolutionary cancer treatment happening on Cape Cod that was reversing glioblastoma and triple-negative breast cancer. Patients were flocking to two pioneering doctors who had revived the Warburg Hypothesis and updated it with protocols and research driven by Thomas Seyfried[2] out of Boston College.

Seyfried had been experimenting with rodents and wrote the book *Cancer as a Metabolic Disease.* The treatments were fairly simple, though completely radical. The theory goes: cells' mitochondria become damaged because of insufficient or damaged respiration, and through a fermentation process, fueled by glucose and glutamine, the damaged cells divide uncontrollably and spread. And, by limiting the cells' access to glucose (sugar and carbs) and glutamine, one could possibly limit the proliferation of these damaged cells by essentially starving them of the fermentable fuels they need.

The human body can survive just fine on non-fermentable fuels—fats and ketone bodies—but cancer cells cannot, so if you convert the human's energy source to fats and ketones the healthy cells are happy and the damaged, cancer cells die. In oversimplified terms: put cancer patients on a ketogenic diet and starve the cells of glucose and see what happens. The theory throws the mainstream idea of cancer as a genetic disease out the window. And since cancer survival rates haven't improved much despite billions spent studying the genes of patients and tumors, many patients agreed it was time for a new approach.

These two doctors were totally overwhelmed with patients who had exhausted all other options and were coming to them desperate for help. Jason, who'd lost both parents to cancer, immediately loved the idea of a show about this new therapy and the patients who were given a second chance at life.

Within months of hearing about Seyfried's research, Jason hopped on a plane to talk with him about his work in rodents. He learned more about why Seyfried thought cancer wasn't actually a genetic disease, but a metabolic disease. The discovery of DNA's structure, by James Watson and Francis Crick in 1953, had inspired the notion that cancer was genetic. But the rates at which patients were dying from cancer had remained pretty much the same—and were arguably even worse, since fewer people were smoking. No cure had been found.

Seyfried used a simple experiment to demonstrate his theory. He explained that when you transfer the nucleus of a healthy cell to a cancer cell, the cancer remains, and when you transfer the nucleus of a cancer cell to healthy cell the cell remains healthy. There is no impact on the health of the cell whether the nucleus (the genetic center) is cancerous or not. Whereas when you transfer the mitochondria of a cancer cell to a healthy cell, you see the cell become cancerous.[3] It is logical to conclude then that the mitochondria are the culprit, not the nucleus. But Seyfried's work was in rodents, and the pioneering doctors on Cape Cod were now experimenting with people.

Jason was sold. He wanted to document what might be the biggest breakthrough in modern medicine. Everyone had been impacted by cancer; the potential audience was massive. And if these doctors on the Cape were successful, his new show could help change the current medical establishment. He called up Michael, a former assistant, and pitched him on the idea. "Well, I can hear the excitement in your voice," Michael said. "But what if it's bullshit? What if this is dangerous and you're promoting it?"

"Well, they've already reversed glioblastoma and triple-negative breast cancer," Jason said. "They're using this guy Seyfried's protocols in Egypt and Turkey. People were going to these countries when they were out of options here. Now, other European governments are looking into it. I think this is going to be massive. Turns out a ton of most hospitals' revenue comes from chemo and radiation, so the financial powers in the U.S. may prevail in keeping this out of the mainstream options. I wouldn't be surprised if we're the last country to adapt these protocols. Hospitals have too much financially at stake."

"Always the cynic, Jason, but I tend to agree—if there's a cheap way to universally treat cancer, people will want to know about it. This show could be bigger than anything we've done before. What is the treatment?" Michael asked.

"It's really simple: the patients get put on a ketogenic diet; given this off-patent drug, costing next to nothing; are treated with hyperbaric oxygen; and put on a fasting schedule. The goal with some patients is simply to stop the spread of the disease; with others, it is to shrink the tumor down to a size that's operable. Like with your brain. If you have a tumor invading various parts of the brain, you're not going to want to cut into it, but if you can reduce the tumor to something small, go in, snip it out, you're saving that person's life."

"Sounds like you're moving to Massachusetts!" Michael said.

"You want to come?" Jason asked. "I don't know a soul there and you'd be a big help on this project. Hiring is going to be tough because I need people who can tell this story without getting too into the weeds. We need both the science and the emotion to come through. I'm worried the hiring will make or break this."

"It's tempting, but you know Kally won't want to leave California," Michael said. "We just got Terrance and Chloe into this private school we love, and I cannot see pulling them out to move east. I wish I could say yes, but I think I'm planted here."

"I was worried you'd say that. Okay, well, who else should I try? Know anyone in New York who'd be willing to trade the Yankees for the Sox?"

"Let me think about it," Michael said before saying goodbye and hanging up the phone.

Within a matter of weeks, Jason had Seyfried and the two doctors on the Cape on the team. They seemed to think the patients would be an easy get, since they were already active on social media about their treatments. But now Jason needed a crew and the production staff to handle it. He was sure he could get the money from investors, but he had no idea what kind of talent he'd find in Boston.

They started shooting before the show was fully staffed—Jason didn't want to miss a single minute of the patients' journeys. While the show was sure to be a hit, life on the Cape in the dead of winter was pretty lonesome. Most of the restaurants were closed for the season. The locals all seemed to be childhood besties and Jason was an obvious outsider. He'd walk into the local diner and people all knew him as the big Hollywood producer. People would smile, but no one ever invited him to Sunday dinner. He longed for coworkers he could call friends.

Staffing *Project Cancer* was the biggest challenge. Jason had some talented college students working as interns, but most of the full-time hires only lasted a year or so. They wanted more of a life than Cape Cod provided them year-round. By its third season, the show was doing really well—it had won an Emmy and calls were coming in from more seasoned television producers looking to join the team.

Now that he had another hit under his belt, Jason could demand the talent he needed. It was also a welcomed change for him personally. Jason was exhausted. He hadn't had a social life apart from a fling with a local hairdresser who he later learned was also dating most of the local volunteer fire department. He missed his friends in LA and he missed the camaraderie they used to have on set of *Golden Ages*.

With the new pool of applicants, he was sure he'd find more of "his people." One candidate for an associate producer position really popped out at him. She had worked in reality TV before but didn't seem to get the hard science stuff, at least not in the interview. That was okay, Jason figured. He never thought he'd be so entrenched in the mitochondrial electron transport chain or the science of oxidative stress. If he could learn all that, she could too. What stood out to him most was her sense of humor. She was a little tough. She pushed back on him and joked a bit during the interview. Jason liked that. He had missed it. Everyone on set seemed to bow to him and that wasn't what he wanted. He wanted to be challenged. He thought Helena was exactly what he'd been missing.

"You follow any sports?" Jason asked on Helena's first day.

"You mean do I like the Dodgers?" she responded. "I mean that's the only team that exists in my world."

"Totally, what a relief, I'm so sick of hearing about the Red Sox."

"Well, you just have to feel bad for 'em, they're still living out their inferiority complex from all those years when they really were losers. Now, they're like those kids whose parents suddenly get rich and they feel like they need to tell everyone how much all their shit costs, so annoying. But hey, you're the one who chose to do this show in Red Sox country."

"Well, I didn't have much of a choice, this is where the doctors were," Jason said with a wink.

"Except you're Jason. I'm pretty sure you could have moved the whole practice to LA. Ever thought of that?"

"I don't know if I could have done that," Jason said with a smile.

"Dude, you're like superman. Don't doubt yourself."

Jason loved having Helena on set. It was refreshing to have her talk back to him, and of course when she complimented him it made him feel great. He thought she was smart and fun. They had great chemistry.

Unfortunately, the third season didn't perform as well as the first two. The audience was getting used to the show's formula: patient comes in on death's door stoop, patient is treated, patient gets better. They needed to mix it up a bit, to tell some surprising stories. Jason gathered the staff for a meeting.

"We're looking at a ratings drop. Cancer is still a killer and our docs are still saving lives, so why aren't we holding our audience? Who has ideas? What elements of these stories will grab people? Let's think of some new angles."

The staff of twenty-five broke into smaller groups and worked on some fresh ideas: follow up with the patients from season one to see how they're doing, tell the stories of the patients' families and partners who are also going through a big ordeal, reach out to the mainstream doctors and see if the show is impacting their practices or making them rethink conventional cancer wisdom. The ideas were all worth testing out with focus groups, but in

Jason's mind, none of them had emerged as a clear winner. He wanted a completely fresh approach. *Golden Ages* had been on the air for six years before the ratings started to drop. Why was this happening so early in the new show's run? He thought back on his hiring options. He'd had such a limited staff and this year was the first year that the gates had opened, and people were willing to relocate. Maybe he hadn't been picky enough.

While he let his staff test out their ideas, he reached out to a few producers he knew in LA: one agreed to come join the team, working as Jason's right hand in every production decision. Etta was a killer producer. Jason knew she'd be a huge asset on staff. She was finishing up a show and would officially start in a month.

Helena was technically a junior staffer, but because she and Jason had a friendship, she had better access to the boss than most. And they texted each other, a lot, which meant she could get an answer from him whenever she wanted.

"You watching this disaster?" Helena texted Jason one night during a Dodgers game.

"Suck my balls, this is awful!" Jason responded.

"No thanks, not tonight," Helena responded with a winky emoji. "Even your balls can't fix this pitching nightmare."

"Why are you awake so late?" Jason asked. "Don't you have to shoot early?"

"Yes, but the new grip invited me out for drinks, and I couldn't say no," Helena responded.

"Are you watching this from a bar?" Jason asked.

"Yup, we convinced the bartender at the Cool Cohog to pop it on."

"Seriously? Great idea!" Jason missed watching baseball in bars. It was one of his favorite things to do in California, but all the local bars were such die-hard Red Sox fans he didn't think watching the Dodgers was an option here.

"Come!!!!!" Helena texted.

"I'd love to another time, but I have to be up early too."

"Oh please, don't be an old man. Get your panties on and come down here. There are four innings left, and it will suck a little less if you're sitting next to me feeling miserable too."

"All right, I'll come, but I'm doing it just for you."

"Cannot wait. You make everything better!"

Their texting was familiar. They were friends. But the power dynamic was omnipresent to Helena. She knew she was texting her boss. She knew he was in charge of her career and she felt being friendly was helpful. But she wasn't interested in him sexually. From Jason's position, he had a friend, an attractive, younger, employee friend. He felt comfortable around her and didn't think so much about the power dynamic.

One night, when they were out drinking, she pitched him on her new idea for the show. "I think we should talk to the doctors' families instead. We're so focused on the patients' perspective, but what about talking with their families, exposing what this has been like for them? Did they think their partners were quacks or were they super onboard from the beginning?"

"That's an interesting angle," Jason said. "I'm not sure that would work. Who are the viewers relating to in that scenario?"

"Well, they're relating to how hard relationships can be," Helena said. "I mean, what if your wife decided to do something radical, and you weren't really onboard, or you were so onboard that you became her cheerleader? I think this may open things up. The docs are central to the show and we don't know a lot about 'em."

"That's true, let me think about it a bit," Jason said. "Want another vodka soda?" He always paid for her drinks.

"Sure, but can we please look into the doctor angle? I'm sure it's gold."

Jason wasn't sure it was gold. In fact, he thought it was kind of a dumb idea. He knew that Helena was better at the emotional side than the science side of the show, but the initial research that had come back seemed to indicate the audience really liked the patient perspective. The reality-TV-show format made it feel accessible to a wide array of viewers, allowing them to gain insight into cancer treatments, including the research as well as the patients' hardships and their resilience. But he wasn't sure that doctors' private lives would add to the show's offerings; he worried it might detract from the main point. The audience needed to trust that the doctors were stable people who were serious about helping cancer patients—if one of them had a bad marriage, that might take over the story line and totally distract from the cancer treatments.

Helena was very serious about her idea. She believed it was what the show needed. Every time she saw Jason on set, she'd ask him: "So you ready to try it out?"

He was annoyed. He didn't want to insult Helena, but he was pretty firm in his resolve that the show was about the patients not the doctors. Telling the doctors' stories would be a completely different kind of show. Jason called up Etta and asked her what she thought.

"Nah, I kind of hate it," Etta responded, in her no-nonsense sort of way. "I mean doctors are always messed-up egomaniacs. It would completely distract from the patient's journey. I think you're just having some growing pains; you don't need to overhaul the whole thing. Just stay true to why this is an important and entertaining concept."

Jason was relieved that Etta had the same reaction he did. The truth was, he'd given Helena's idea way more time than any of the others because he personally liked her. They were on the same page on most stuff, but not this.

The next time he saw her, he said, "I've thought a lot about your idea and I see why it's interesting, but it's not the right move for us, not now."

"What? No way. Seriously? It's like the best idea anyone has come up with. Are you serious?" Helena was obviously upset.

"Yeah, I mean it's nothing personal, but we don't need to completely overhaul the concept, and frankly, doctors are often messy characters, which can work in some shows, but this one is about the patients."

"Right, and people are sick of the patients. We need a little mess," Helena said.

She was overstepping and Jason wished she'd cool it. He didn't want to have to verbally pull rank, but this idea of hers wasn't going anywhere. It was getting a little awkward.

"You know, I think it might be a cool spin-off show, or something." Jason was grasping for some way to soothe Helena but also communicate that her idea wasn't going to happen. "You know, I think the Sox are playing tonight. Want to go grab some drinks and root for a loss?"

"Yeah, no thanks," Helena said and walked away. He felt like she was mad at him.

By the time that Etta arrived on set, there were rumors floating around that Helena and Jason had broken up. Etta hated gossip.

"Were you shtupping that AP?" she asked Jason.

"What!? No!" he said.

"Well, your whole crew thinks you were and that you broke her heart. Lots of pissed-off people."

"Seriously, I never hooked up with her. We're friends."

"No, I don't think so. I think she thought it was more."

"Why? We watched baseball and joked around, I never tried to kiss her or anything."

"Did you text her about your balls? Did you drink alcohol with her? Did you pay for her drinks and take her out all the time? Text her about nonwork stuff late at night?"

"Yeah, I guess, but it wasn't weird. . . . I'm not a creep." Jason was now thinking back to all the jokes he'd made and all the late-night confessions about ex-girlfriends. Oh my god, was Helena sharing those with his crew? Was the whole set buzzing about his past heartbreaks? What a betrayal of their friendship.

"What do I do?" Jason asked Etta.

"I think you'd better do nothing. This could get worse fast. I guess my first job is going to be cleaning up this mess."

"I didn't mean to do anything wrong. I thought we were friends. I hired her because I liked bantering with her. What a shitshow."

"Right, so here's the thing, you aren't really ever 'friends' with anyone you're hiring to work for you. They can't be completely honest with you. I mean you know this, right? You are the boss. You are a powerful person in this industry. Have you been living in a cave? You cannot go out drinking with younger members of this staff, men or women. It's not okay. You may feel comfortable with them, because they don't have any power over you or your livelihood or your future career. They screw up at work, you replace them. But flip that shit and think if one of them offended you. What if one of them said something that you really hated, or that made you question their moral character? You'd probably fire them, right? That means they're always on guard around you, always. Which means you have the power. The power to promote them, to fire them, to help them land another job with a bigger show, to blackball them from the industry. They have a lot on the line here. You are not equals. You therefore cannot be friends. That power imbalance doesn't disappear when you drive off the set, nor does it disappear when you text late at night. If your best friend texts you some stupid joke in the middle of the night, you will probably ignore it and answer in the morning. BUT if your boss sends you a text in the middle of the night, you're going to answer it. That's what I mean. Not equals. You cannot be friends if you're not equals."

> ∨ *You aren't really ever "friends" with anyone you're*
> ∨ *hiring to work for you. They can't be completely*
> ∨ *honest with you. I mean you know this, right?*
> ∨ *You are the boss.*

Jason had to think about it. He knew that on many levels Etta was right. But he was upset he'd been so blind to it. Loneliness had taken over and his judgement had lapsed. Certainly, he wasn't the only person working in a remote location who'd hired someone hoping they'd become friends, but it would be the last time he'd do it.

Etta was able to talk to Helena and learned that her feelings had been hurt when her proposal was dismissed. She had thought of Jason as a friend but certainly not an equal. She kind of had a crush on him, it seemed. When she was upset and a cameraman asked what was wrong, she overshared. She explained she had feelings for a guy that she knew was out of her league, and that she felt like a fool. The cameraman in turn deduced that she was talking about Jason and asked Helena if he'd ever led her on. She shared some of the texts they'd sent, not to tattle, but to confirm that they'd been flirting. The cameraman concurred, but privately voiced his concerns to Etta. "Seemed sad," he said. "Like this sweet kid got wrapped up in the whole big man, big power, big show, bright future kind of stuff. Not great, but you know who's to blame?"

Helena wound up leaving the production and heading back home. She was sad things had ended that way, but she felt rejected and couldn't really recover while still working for Jason. He also felt rejected. He'd wanted to have a friend at work and he really liked Helena. But he'd missed the power element. He learned a few hard lessons; don't hire people you want to be friends with and don't be overly friendly with your subordinates. It can get messy really fast. For Jason, who loved to joke around, that meant he wouldn't go out drinking with his staffers and he wouldn't text people after hours about non-work-related topics. Those rules kept things clean and saved him from having to worry.

> ⌄ *He learned a few hard lessons; don't hire people you*
> ⌄ *want to be friends with and don't be overly friendly*
> ⌄ *with your subordinates. It can get messy really fast.*

Key Takeaways

Hiring for you rather than for the role:

- If you've done what we've suggested earlier in this book, you will feel connected to the applicant you offer the job to, but be very aware that you do not want to hire exclusively on this connection. You need to know the person can do the job and that there is no confusion for them or you about why they were hired and what their role within the organization will be.
- The boss test: remember, if you wouldn't say it to your boss or your child's teacher you probably shouldn't say it to someone who you have the power to fire. The power imbalance is felt acutely, and it can build resentment, or worse still, lead to legal action.
- You should not be scared to mentor or hire women, that is not the lesson in this story. It doesn't matter what the gender is of the person below you on the chain of command. Everyone deserves respect, and everyone knows you're the boss. Set the tone and assume those below you do not think of you as an equal, so you should not view them that way either.

THIRTEEN

Value People Who Are Egotistical and Primarily Interested in Their Own Future

Tyrone's* resume was fantastic. He'd worked in the private sector and in government, and his connections were exactly what this communications firm needed. In a recent meeting a client, who had worked with Tyrone before, had slipped his resume to a manager, who'd sent it along up the chain until it landed on Milly's* desk. She was excited to interview him.

The position was sensitive because it involved many ex-politicians who were now on the book circuit. They had massive egos and needed constant soothing. The right candidate would understand this and not take it personally when the clients' hissy fits hit the fan, which they were sure to do. Confidentiality was also a must, since the firm's reputation was built on trust and the ability to delicately manage the egos who ran the world.

Specifically, Milly had a client with a memoir due out in just four months. It had been a miracle that they'd survived the writing process. While they weren't involved in any of the writing itself, they were copied on all the correspondence. Government employees seemed to think that the more people copied on a message, the more shame fell on its subject. However, in most instances, the cc'd parties privately commiserated with one another and joked about the sender's immaturities. This case was no exception.

It was tough to find the right people for these roles. Often, someone would come in with one of the necessary characteristics, but not the others. It was always stressful when someone left the firm because replacements were a tough find.

Tyrone seemed to fit the bill better than most and Milly hoped the interview would be a breeze. While the comms managers primarily put out fires, they were sometimes asked to ghostwrite or be the client's impromptu spokesperson. That meant Milly needed to test Tyrone on his abilities to perform under pressure. She welcomed him into her corner office.

"Hi there, please have a seat," Milly said, her assistant closing the door behind Tyrone.

"Wow, what a great office," Tyrone said, looking out her floor-to-ceiling windows.

"Thanks. So, tell me a bit about yourself, Tyrone," Milly started.

"Sure, so I've been in the Beltway for about a decade and I love it. Love the power, love the hunger here, you know, the behind-the-scenes stuff. Love it all."

"Sure, it's the center of the world they say, but tell me what it is about the power you love?"

"I think being close to power is exciting, I like knowing that I'm contributing, helping to move the needle."

Milly liked his answers; he would likely be working with a former president, and feeling comfortable with that level of authority was important. She wanted to know more. Milly was a trained CIA analyst and she was hired in large part because of her ability to get people to open up. For this position, she needed to know that the applicants thought of themselves as an extension of the client. It was more important that they showed they were collaborators rather than competitors. Everyone signed NDAs, but the truth was a lucrative book deal could cover the cost of damages so the contract was hardly a perfect preventative measure. And then there were the disgruntled employees who sought vengeance by leaking embarrassing stories to the press.

"Have you ever been in a position where things went south, or when your idea wasn't accepted? How did that go?" Milly pushed.

"You know, not for a while," Tyrone said confidently. "Maybe when I was younger and learning how to manage egos and working on my own, but not in the last five years or so. I think most of my ideas are pretty well-received."

It was an interesting answer. On the one hand Milly respected it if it was true. Often great employees feel like they need to temper themselves to appear more self-aware or offer examples of humility. But there was something about Tyrone's last statement that felt to Milly's keen ears slightly defensive.

"Well, that's impressive," she said, hoping to calm his flare of insecurity if that's what it was, because now, she'd need to dig a little deeper. "So, tell me a bit about the mistakes other people have made."

"Ha, that's a great question," Tyrone said falling face-first into Milly's trap. "I think I see a lot of people who are powerful, but maybe not well-rounded. I'd like to think I can offer that. I'm pretty good at a lot of things, you know, Milly. I like to learn and that makes me knowledgeable and when people get to know me it becomes clear that I'm worth listening to, so when they don't listen to me they're telling me a lot about themselves."

Milly immediately sensed the irony: he was telling her a lot about himself. "Right, I completely agree," she said. "So when have you worked with someone powerful who wasn't wellrounded?"

"I once had this boss who was so full of himself, he would tell us all to send him weekly progress reports and in them list five things he'd done to help us, as a kind of reminder to him and I guess to us that he was helpful. It was a complete ego trip. I thought it was ridiculous. I would have liked to list five things that I'd done that helped him."

"That's an interesting approach," Milly noted, intentionally not saying whether she was referring to Tyrone's approach or his boss's.

"Yeah, I like to help, but you know we all like to get credit for our help too," Tyrone said.

Milly immediately recognized he'd assumed her feedback was directed at him, not his former boss. As a rule of thumb, Milly didn't think it was a good sign when an interviewee mentioned something negative about their old employer. If asked, most people can come up with something they didn't like about a boss, but volunteering that information was a completely different matter. It told her that the candidate tends to blame others and isn't self-aware about who they're speaking to, which immediately makes the potential employer wonder if the candidate will speak about them this way too.

"Have you had other bosses whom you've had a hard time getting along with?" Milly asked.

"I get along with my bosses," Tyrone retorted. "I just don't always think they're great leaders. That's an important difference."

"I see," Milly said. She was going to remain quiet for as long as she could stand. She knew that this awkward pause would result in Tyrone sharing more. She looked down at her notes. Then her eyes locked on his. His face looked tenser than it had a few minutes earlier. Milly told herself to silently count to thirty and wait.

"I think I'll learn a lot here," he burst out. "I said before, I like to learn and I think this will be a great place to learn."

He was turning the conversation to a more positive topic, which was good. But Milly didn't love that he was still talking about himself. I love, I want, I'm good at, and so on all signaled that he was thinking exclusively about his own experience. Instead of thinking about what he could contribute to the company, what his involvement would do for them, he was focused on his future and his needs. This was a turnoff. Milly was determined not to respond.

When working in intelligence, she'd learned the art of not showing emotions in an interview. Humans are profoundly adept at reading each other's facial expressions and body language. The micro expressions documented by Paul Ekman and others only scratch the surface of the various nonverbal ways we communicate. Learning to control your face, hands, and other body parts is like unlearning how to talk. It's hard, but powerful.

> ∨ *The micro expressions documented by Paul Ekman*
> ∨ *and others only scratch the surface of the various*
> ∨ *nonverbal ways we communicate. Learning to control*
> ∨ *your face, hands, and other body parts is like*
> ∨ *unlearning how to talk. It's hard, but powerful.*

Milly sat looking directly at Tyrone, not communicating anything. "I feel like what I really need is a challenge. I want to make a difference and I want to help, but in the past, I haven't been challenged enough. I have been limited. I think if I got the job here, I would be challenged. I mean you've already made me think more in this interview than I did in like three years at my past job." When Tyrone finished his soliloquy, he was sure Milly would respond, but she didn't. He was doing exactly what she wanted, he was oversharing. This is where she'd really get to know who Tyrone was. It's human nature to want an awkward silence to go away, and people often fill the void with their deepest thoughts.

"I'm not saying I didn't think at that job." Tyrone was now aware of his verbal diarrhea. He tried to be quiet, but then he felt he needed to explain. "I sometimes feel like I do better under pressure, and when the pressure lets up, I guess I let up a bit too. I have this tendency to want to prove myself and I seem to do that when I feel I've been misunderstood, or like someone doesn't think I can do something. I want to prove them wrong, you know?"

Tyrone was desperate for Milly to react.

"I'm aware that I'm talking too much," he said, looking for a rescue. "I'm not sure why I'm saying all of this. What was your original question?"

He now felt very self-conscious. This was a job interview, not a shrink appointment. Now that he'd asked Milly a direct question, she felt obligated to answer.

"I think I asked you about how other people had made mistakes," she said. "Do you want to talk more about what pushes you to perform?"

"No," Tyrone said. "I think I've overshared already."

"Not at all," Milly said. "I want to get to know you. Tell me a little more about why you want to work here."

"You all have the best reputation," he said. "I know this would be great experience for me. As I blurted out a minute ago, I think I'd be pushed here and that I'd learn a lot. I love that you all have such phenomenal clients. I love that I'd get to work with some of the most powerful people in the world, to help them shape their message, to clean up their messes. All of that, all of it. My goal is to one day start my own firm, something small, not like this, but a boutique, bespoke comms firm and working here would be amazing preparation for that goal."

Milly had heard it all before. The "I" story. She understood why this job would be good for him, but he hadn't said much about why it would be good for the firm. All too often people came in who seemed well-qualified but then the entire interview focused on their needs and wants and not what they were going to offer. Milly wondered if there was some self-help book out there telling people to talk about themselves this way. Like when people repeat your name over and over as if to say, "Look, see? I

remember your name," or "Pay attention; I'm saying your name."
Both approaches were a mistake.

If he'd reframed his points and spoken about how he wanted to
offer the firm his deep knowledge of how government worked or
that he wanted to use his connections to secure speaking gigs for
clients or any other contribution Milly was sure he could make, she
would have been more impressed. Instead his exclusive interest in
his own goals left her wondering about his commitment. It wasn't
a deal breaker to say that you eventually wanted to branch out on
your own, but to do it in the context of acquiring skills and connections at the firm's cost wasn't the right way to position it.

When Milly walked Tyrone to the door, she wished him well
and said they'd be in touch. She was on the fence for so many
reasons—after all, he had the qualifications for the job. But there
was something lingering in the back of her mind about his motivations and his drive. She understood he was competitive and
appreciated his insights into why he needed to feel challenged.
Milly also knew that sometimes when people describe needing a
challenge what they really meant was that they needed an adver-
sary. They needed someone who didn't believe in them, who
asked too much of them, who was mean or critical. People respond to that kind of pressure in three ways: they crumble; they
rise to the occasion with a chip on their shoulder; or, best-case
scenario, they grow by getting the work done and building a
solid, new, respectful relationship. But the latter is the rarest case.
When you know you're most likely to need someone who can go
up against a challenge more than someone who needs it, it's a
tough call to hire someone you know might like to fight.

Great achievements can come from competition between ad-
versaries, but this wasn't the kind of work culture Milly had tried

to create. The firm was almost the antithesis of it—it worked hard to bring people together, to solve conflicts, and encourage collaboration. Her reading on Tyrone was that while he was a great dog to have in a fight, you wouldn't ever want to be in a fight with him.

When she shared her feedback with her boss, who usually didn't weigh in on manager roles, Robert wanted to meet Tyrone. When they brought him back in for a second interview, he invited a few colleagues to join him. Group interviews were intense. The applicant was expected to look at the panel of esteemed communication executives and keep their cool. It was nearly impossible to prepare properly, since they didn't know exactly who would be present. In Tyrone's case, there was Robert, who was a senior partner at the firm; Kate, the head of crisis management; Sidney, the head of legal; and Milly, who was back to observe. They sat on one side of a gigantic conference room table and Tyrone sat on the other side, closest to the door. It was a power play, but it was also how a lot of their client meetings went. The client would show up with a couple lawyers, a private publicist, sometimes a family member or even a friend, and the manager would have to face the whole squad.

Tyrone settled into his chair. He looked prepared, with a big smile on his face and a yellow legal pad and a fancy silver pen in front of him. He wasn't sure what he'd need to take notes on, but he thought it would make him look ready for anything.

"Tyrone, welcome back, we're looking forward to talking with you a bit more," Milly said. "I'm going to help facilitate this interview, which should take about one hour, but since you've already answered my questions, I will turn things over to Robert."

"Hello, Tyrone, I hear great things about you," Robert said. "You come from McSteevey, a great firm. I once had an internship there, way back when dinosaurs roamed the earth." Robert was a well-known talker and was clearly trying to set an informal tone. "You know Spencer Plow? He still over there?"

"No, I don't think I do. Sorry, I guess I haven't had the pleasure," Tyrone said.

"Ah, he's the man—used to be my tennis partner before my knee crapped out. Great guy. I think he's in risk management there; you ever deal with that department?"

"Well, I've had touch points with them, sure, but mostly over emails, you know, like back and forth on drafts before they're released. I don't really know anyone in that department."

"I see, okay, well enough with the name game," Robert said. "Tell me what you like about our firm."

"Well, I like a lot of things," Tyrone started. "I like that it's an incredible institution, built on trust and expertise. I would be honored to work here with you all and with your talented, incredible clients. I think I'd grow a lot and I'm sure I'd learn a ton. It seems like a beautiful space to work in and everyone has been so friendly to me."

As Tyrone talked, all Milly heard was "me" and "I" over and over. This was making her feel like her gut on Tyrone was right. He was perhaps a little immature and self-centered. Those two qualities didn't work well at this firm. She needed to know her managers were 100 percent about their clients. When the shit hit the fan, they needed to act quickly and make the right choices for their clients or risk losing them and damaging the firm's reputation. It was a tall order.

"Tell me about a time when you weren't proud of your work," Sidney asked.

"Well, I think you're the head of legal here, so let me start by saying I have not been in any legal trouble." Tyrone was trying to banter, but Sidney was dead serious.

"Good to know, but I'm more interested in how you approach problems and what happens when your approach doesn't pan out the way you'd hoped," Sidney clarified. She would of course have her department run a full background check on Tyrone if they decided to offer him the job, but she wasn't going to discuss any of her procedures or share what she might be able to find with Tyrone at this stage—or likely ever.

"I think I've been pretty lucky. I mean maybe it hasn't been luck, maybe I've just been good at making the right choices, but there haven't been a lot of mistakes in my past. I think Milly asked me something similar and I told her, honestly, I don't know. Sure, there have been times when I've worked hard on something and the team came together, but it didn't result in a big win, but I still learned and grew from those experiences, so in my mind they were still wins. I think I try to look at everything as an opportunity. If I fall on my face, I get back up and look at what went wrong and then I don't make that same mistake again. So, you know, I don't really look at those missteps as failures. I look at them as a chance to grow."

It was a great response, but it didn't actually answer Sidney's question. She wasn't interested in his philosophical stance on resilience, she wanted to know when and where and how he'd messed up.

"That's great, but can you give me some examples? When have you not accomplished your goals and had to pick yourself back up?" Sidney wasn't going to let him off the hook so easily. Her job was to assess Tyrone's truthfulness. She was a legal expert. She was also a deceit expert and her role at the firm was equal parts to protect the clients and her employer. Her loyalty wasn't to any one person, but to the firm itself. Sidney could recognize deflection a mile away and that's exactly what Tyrone was doing.

"So specifically, let me think," Tyrone said. Sidney watched him and instantly saw inside Tyrone's head: he was thinking of all the times he'd come in second place. Tyrone watched a montage of past failures flicker by and sorted through them, hoping to land on one that satisfied the questions but didn't disqualify him for the job. Like when an interviewer asks an applicant what their worst quality is, every prepared candidate responds with, "I work too hard." Finding the right answer is the key, Tyrone thought.

"This is a bit embarrassing." Tyrone was setting the stage, building anticipation with a dash of humility. "I was working for Secretary of State Flinton, and I was charged with ordering food for her birthday. I know she likes chocolates, we kept them in jars all over the office, so I assumed she'd like chocolate cake, with chocolate frosting. I mean who doesn't like chocolate cake, especially from A Baked Joint off K Street. I had personalized M&Ms with her initials scattered on all the tabletops. It was going to be great. But when the secretary arrived, she was with a major donor to her campaign for Senate a decade ago. Well, he's apparently a diabetic and is involved in a massive lawsuit against some big-time candy makers over their targeted marketing, which he thinks is making kids sick and more likely to develop Type II diabetes. It was a whole thing. We had to sweep all the custom M&Ms into waste bins and desk drawers and even under desks as fast as we could. We had to try to get a diabetic-approved cake at the very least minute."

"The secretary was a good sport, but it was a blunder on my part. I didn't have access to her calendar, and no one told me she was bringing anyone. I guess the meeting had been added weeks before, but no one mentioned it to me. It was embarrassing. It also stunk because I'd worked hard on all the prep and got like zero credit for it. But I think in the end no real damage was done. Other than maybe to the vacuum, which was full of M&Ms."

Robert laughed. Sidney wrote some notes. Milly couldn't help but hear how he only quasi took responsibility, and Kate was clearly evaluating the risk Tyrone took by not checking the calendar ahead of time.

"So, do you consider yourself a risk taker?" Kate chimed in with a smile.

"No, ma'am," Tyrone said. "I do not like risks. I prefer to stay in my lane and do as I'm told. In this case, I was told to get refreshments for a birthday party. To be honest, I thought I was being very safe. I mean, who would serve fruit and veggies at a birthday party on the Hill? No one, that's who! In general, I like to pick the path of least resistance; I do not like to ruffle feathers."

Kate liked his answer. She thought he seemed charming and well-adjusted. He answered all their questions and was clearly excited about the opportunity.

After the interview the four executives gathered to compare their notes. Milly, as the head of HR, led the discussion. "Remember, do not bring up any personal information that might be perceived as a bias or a persuasion. We are simply evaluating Tyrone on the merits of his CV and his answers here today. Now that I've gotten that out of the way, what did you all think?"

"Milly, what were your thoughts?" Robert asked. "Before I chime in I'd like to hear how your feelings have changed or stayed the same?"

"I think I feel the same as I did after the first interview," she said. "I think he seems qualified, but I have some reservations about his self-centeredness. He didn't take responsibility for the M&M debacle, and while that is not a major incident it could have been. Imagine if he was careless like that with Charlie Price. He's so protective of his brand and would flip if he came in here and we tried to serve him a competitor's soda. That attention to detail is everything in a manager. I also think he is mostly interested in bettering his own career, rather than contributing meaningfully here. Just my gut, but I clearly have some reservations."

"I think that's overdoing it," Robert said. "Does anyone else feel like this guy isn't right?"

"I share in some of the concerns Milly expressed," Sidney said. "I feel he dodged our questions a bit and he certainly didn't share anything that gave us a real look into how he's learned from mistakes or what errors he might make again and what he struggles with. That's leaving me feeling like I just don't know. He could be great, he could be not great."

"You two using your mental telepathy to get this info? I didn't get any of that," Robert retorted. "He seems fantastic. Funny as hell. I mean that M&M business was straight outta *Veep*. I like that kind of stuff, shows you can get along and we all know getting along is a key to this business. Kate, thoughts?"

"I thought he seemed adequate," Kate said. As a risk assessor she didn't mince words—she wasn't a fan of being too complimentary or too negative.

"That's all?" Robert pushed.

"I think he seems young, maybe a bit immature. I felt he'd gotten some coaching on the interview, which I see as good. I don't think coaches actually help to change who you are or win anyone over, but it does show a commitment, a drive, and an investment in the process. It shows he wants the job, or at the very least he wants a new job. I thought his M&M story was a good example to pull out. I also agree with Milly that he mentioned himself a few too many times. I tend to be more forgiving about that stuff, because he's young and he could be coached out of that."

With two executives for hiring Tyrone and two with reservations, the call fell to Robert. He decided Tyrone's humor won him the position. He certainly had the experience and Robert felt his personal style was an asset, not a detraction.

But that was a mistake. A few months into the job, Tyrone had become a drain on office morale. Everyone normally enjoyed joking together and the atmosphere was generally positive, but Tyrone had a habit of stirring up criticisms about things that wouldn't have otherwise become a big deal. He would point out where someone had fallen short or when a client was being a pain in the ass.

The firm worked best when everyone pitched in because sometimes an employee would need to attend to a personal matter or they weren't their best selves, but as a team they could support one another. Tyrone didn't share this work ethic. Instead, he'd blame others, complain that he was being held back, and that people were out to get him. This made everyone else defensive and opened the floodgates so that others complained about Tyrone in a retaliatory manner.

Tyrone had a similar way with clients. He was charming to their face but behind their backs he seemed resentful of their power. It was as if he thought they should be working for him, when in fact he was clearly the subordinate in the relationship. It was subtle, but his negative attitude dragged down all of the teams he was on.

Milly and Sidney had been right. The personal "I" stance that Tyrone displayed in the interview had been symptomatic of his positional approach to everything. His downfall would be his inability to get out of his own way. Tyrone was very smart. He was capable. Robert and Kate were attracted to his humor and his successful track record, but in the end those traits weren't enough to overcome the deeply rooted insecurities that caused him to make everything about him. This prevented Tyrone from accepting feedback that might have otherwise been an opportunity for growth.

While it is hard to fire someone for having a bad attitude, it is harder still to diagnose how toxic a self-centered person can be to an organization on a systemic level. But damage is done when someone isn't a team player, when they don't take responsibility for their actions, and when they aren't up for helping out a coworker who needs support.

ⱽ *While it is hard to fire someone for having a bad*
ⱽ *attitude, it is harder still to diagnose how toxic a*
ⱽ *self-centered person can be to an organization*
ⱽ *on a systemic level. But damage is done when*
ⱽ *someone isn't a team player, when they don't take*
ⱽ *responsibility for their actions, and when they aren't*
ⱽ *up for helping out a coworker who needs support.*

Key Takeaways

- When you interview someone who uses the first-person "I" to talk about what they want, need, and hope for without also talking about what they can contribute, take a second to assess whether this person is going to be a drain on your organization.

- Look for people who talk about wanting to solve the problems your company is working on. That shows an investment in your mission, rather than a personal goal.

- When a candidate blames others for past mistakes, they might not have learned the lessons they could have. Look for people who take responsibility for their actions and who can talk about growing from hardship.

- When a candidate insults a former boss or employer it should be seen as a red flag. Either they are not aware of their audience, or they are trying to bond with you by celebrating someone else's flaws or failings. This is likely a pattern of behavior that the person will replicate in your office, and it can be quite divisive.

- Job candidates are often told to be professional and confident. Maybe people do not realize that confidence is not about bragging or sounding self-assured: it is about taking ownership and responsibility and knowing who you are so you can calculate risk-reward accurately. Because many people aren't working off of the right definition, be gentle in your analysis. Try asking open-ended questions to get the applicant to talk about their experiences in a less scripted way so that you can learn their true character. Just as you wouldn't want to hire an egomaniac, you also need to be aware of candidates who've been over-coached. When someone sounds too scripted or your intuition tells you they aren't being authentic, find a new line of questioning. Remember, many people go to coaches who teach them how not to be themselves. This is a mistake. Sometimes you can break through the coaching, sometimes you can't, but it is worth trying to dig a little deeper.

- The goal of the interview must be to get to know the person. In order to do that, you must make them comfortable and you must ask the right questions at the right time.

FOURTEEN

Cindy Brown's Lesson in Adapting with the Times[1]

Boston Duck Tours are legendary. The amphibious vehicles offer tourists and residents a chance to see the city by land and water. With character guides like Plucky Ruffles who looks like Elvis but sounds like a Harvard PhD in colonial history, guests are entertained and enlightened.

Cindy Brown, an owner who has been at the famous Boston Duck Tours since inception, told me in an interview that if she were a guide, she'd be "Jane Funda." She'd wear a fun leotard with leggings and be a workout-style Boston historian. She wants to hire high-quality people who love what they do. And hiring is a huge part of her job, because her staff includes everyone from office managers to mechanics to historians, so there is no one-size-fits-all approach.

In addition to the difficulties of staffing such varied roles, the company also faces the challenges of seasonal tourism. From March to November their employees are working long days and expected to have a positive, customer-facing attitude at all times. Ticket sellers need to be approachable, responsible, and representative of the brand, while the guides need to be captivating and articulate for every ride. Dependent on people not getting sick, not quitting, and returning season after season is a tall order, but one that Brown manages. After all, imagine the nightmare she'd face if she were forced to hire all new employees each season.

She says one of the tricks to retaining most of the staff is offering them health insurance in the off season. If employees don't return to work when the season starts back up, then they have to reimburse Boston Duck Tours for the full cost of their health care. If employees return, then they only owe the standard 20 percent copay—Boston Duck Tours covers the rest. This is enough of an incentive to keep most of the talent onboard through the winter.

Brown says the challenges of the job are what keep her interested, but there are times when she has had to change company policies in ways that she doesn't love. For example, when a law passed demanding that new mothers and fathers be given the same amount of parental leave, Brown had to scale back her maternity leave. Before the law passed, she had offered female employees six weeks' leave. But because more than 80 percent of her employees are men, there was no way that she could afford to give six weeks of paid time off to everyone, she said. Now, Brown can only offer one week of paid parental leave, which bothers her deeply. But these are the unintended consequences of the legislation that small businesses must deal with.

The changes in parental leave laws did not represent the first time Brown had to learn to adapt her hiring practices in the face of changing legislation. With each new restriction, she has found a way to keep the company afloat. But after a fatal accident involving a pedestrian in 2016, a new law was enacted that forced her company to overhaul its employment strategy completely.

The family of the woman who was killed, struck by the Duck while on a scooter, called for new regulations for all amphibious vehicles. The new law required drivers to focus exclusively on the road, while a separate person entertained the passengers. The hope was that this would cut down on distracted driving and therefore cut down on accidents. But the law only impacted amphibious vehicles, which meant that double-decker buses, trolley cars, and other tour companies did not have to change their operations. This limited application of the law and exceptions made for other tour companies implied the new law was directed specifically at the Ducks.

Brown could have contested it on a number of grounds, not least of which was that it made these exceptions for other vehicles. Instead she welcomed the new safety regulations, hoping they would help in the aftermath of the tragedy. But this also meant that the Boston company would have to completely overhaul its balance sheet.

"We chose to do what we thought was the right thing to do," Brown said. "It cost our company a *ton* of money. It cut into our profits hugely, but we think it's the best solution."

As Brown explained, the new law didn't just mean hiring another person. Staffing each Duck with two staffers rather than one increased all costs associated with labor—not just payroll. Making matters worse, it is not easy to find seasonal drivers. Finding the right people with excellent driving records and all of the qualifications Brown demands of those responsible for the Ducks is tough.

"We had to hire like 60 new people, so we went from basically 150 employees to over 200," Brown said. "We had to have space for them, and we had to have trainers for them. We had to have uniforms for them. We have benefits for them. We have paid for that. We had to have everything grow exponentially in two months. We needed more managers to manage them. We went from part-time HR to full-time HR. We added two more operations managers. We had such a buildup, which is why we couldn't just do it overnight and find these people. And even to this day, when we're on our third year in, we still are not staffed fully because we can't find enough drivers. Every single year we've had that problem. Again, I'm not disappointed with the decision. I think it was the right decision, but it's been really hard to fill our needs based upon having that many more employees."

And the costs from the huge increase in hiring have come exclusively out of Brown's and the Boston Duck Tours' investors' wallets.

"We never took a penny from anyone's bonus," Brown said. "We never took a penny from anyone's annual pay increases. Everyone is still making the same or more per hour. The investors, myself included, took the entire hit of those millions of dollars in losses because we were not going to say, oh, because we have to hire more people, now everyone's going to make less."

It's clear that as the job market has tightened, it's become harder for Brown to find qualified people to help her run the

Duck Tours. She estimates that 50 percent of the people they reach out to for interviews don't show up and many of those who do aren't dressed appropriately. She needs to know that the people she hires are trustworthy and responsible, and if you show up to an interview in workout clothes, you're not sending the message that you're serious about the position. Even though her hands are tied in many ways, Brown will continue to adapt the business because she enjoys these kinds of challenges—they've kept her interested twenty-five years into starting this national phenomenon.

"Every year there's new challenges and there's new legislation, or there's nuances to running a business that I can work on that keeps me interested."

> ∨ *She needs to know that the people she hires are*
> ∨ *trustworthy and responsible, and if you show up*
> ∨ *to an interview in workout clothes, you're not*
> ∨ *sending the message that you're serious about the*
> ∨ *position. Even though her hands are tied in many*
> ∨ *ways, Brown will continue to adapt the business*
> ∨ *because she enjoys these kinds of challenges—*
> ∨ *they've kept her interested twenty-five years into*
> ∨ *starting this national phenomenon.*

Key Takeaways

Adaptation is key to survival.

- Always be aware of how changes in the environment may impact your hiring practices.
- Come up with creative workarounds when you're faced with hiring challenges—like offering health insurance in the offseason.
- Think of the big picture, face your critics, and work together on solutions.
- Do your best to make your working space fun and restore some autonomy to the staff. Letting drivers pick their names, costumes, and personalities surely makes the job more fun for each individual.

FIFTEEN

There's Nothing Wrong with Nepotism

Family businesses used to form the foundation of the U.S. economy. Your dad would start a business and eventually he brought in his brothers, then you and your siblings. The family business was a source of stable income, and in many ways, that was the best protection you could provide for your loved ones and future generations.

But things changed after World War II, and since then, we have seen the almighty mega-corporation take over as the fuel for the American economy. Today, fewer and fewer Americans believe they can rise up on their own and provide for themselves. Increased taxes and regulations have strangled small businesses in favor of multinational corporations, which have established a

massive influence campaign through lobbying and political do-
nations. With *Burwell v. Hobby Lobby Stores* in 2014, the U.S.
granted corporations the same "right" as individual citizens, a
landmark case that forever changed the power dynamics of
American businesses.

So, when we talk about nepotism, it's no longer within the
framework of a father who wants his son to inherit the family
business. Those situations are outliers. More likely, a father running a company would hire his kids, his friends' kids, or his kids'
friends, granting them access to positions that would allow them
to build wealth and power.

Hiring managers should be wary of these kinds of pressures.
It builds a rotten culture based on favors and faulty expectations.
It steals the respect from those who have actually earned their
positions, and frankly, the lucky few who are able to skip the
hiring line don't feel great about their positions either. When it
was more like inheritance, nepotism may have had a more important function, but now that most companies are mammoths,
the idea that someone's kid should get favorable treatment
doesn't hold up.

∨   *When it was more like inheritance, nepotism may*
∨   *have had a more important function, but now that*
∨   *most companies are mammoths, the idea that*
∨   *someone's kid should get favorable treatment*
∨   *doesn't hold up.*

Greta* was the daughter of Stella, the CMO of Bullseye, a
major retail chain. When she graduated from Brown, she got a
job at an MMMB, a discount retailer with a significant footprint

that offered a highly valued training program. When Greta completed her training, she was off to Harvard Business School. And when she graduated with an MBA, her mom knocked down the doors of Bullseye to get her a mid-level position in the online marketing department.

The application process was simple: Stella brought Greta's resume to Robin, the VP of online marketing, who was Stella's direct report, and told her Greta had "some terrific ideas about how to increase their online traffic." The interviews were all great. Greta was certainly qualified, had glowing references, and was ready to start. Nothing seemed too far out of line. Robin notified HR that Greta was her first choice. They felt comfortable with the decision, having publicly posted the job and conducted other interviews, so they weren't concerned that the hiring situation was legally unfair.

But therein lies the dilemma. When an employee's child is unqualified for the position, things are much more clear-cut—everyone involved knows that something unfair is afoot. In these instances, people either go along with it because the political pressure is too great to challenge, or they suggest an alternative position. The mailroom has a reputation for being the right entry-level gig for the children of executives. But what about when the executive's child is qualified? Is there any reason to second guess the choice?

> ∨ *The mailroom has a reputation for being the right*
> ∨ *entry-level gig for the children of executives. But*
> ∨ *what about when the executive's child is qualified?*

There is an old adage that in family businesses the first generation creates the opportunities, the second generation builds and grows the base business beyond first generation's expectations, and the third generation doesn't want to work for the business at all. This trajectory has everything to do with earned respect and is fundamental to hiring the right people for the right jobs. Most people do not want to be put in a position just because their family expects them to do the job. No one wants to be less successful than their parents. Nearly everyone wants the autonomy to choose what they do with their life, and most people want to feel connected to their work. The third generation—not to mention the people who believe they unfairly got the job—do not feel satisfied working in an expected role because of every one of these factors.

If we expand on the family business adage, we can see how important identity is to shaping roles. Let's imagine that the true entrepreneur was the first-generation family member. They built something from nothing. Their children likely witnessed their hard work and grit, often in the face of financial and personal risk. Watching their parents' dedication and commitment was intoxicating. Their children want to be a part of what their parents had built. In reality, kids want to help their parents as much as parents want to help their kids. This is a naturally occurring phenomenon. In the enterprise's infancy, those second-generation kids were probably expected to help out with the business while they were growing up and in turn developed a personal connection and sense of pride for their contributions.

By the time the second generation takes over, they've inherited a successful business. This generation is now in a position where they can expand the company, take on new risk, and turn a small operation into something more significant. These executives have insight into the company's founding mission, why the company was a success, the risks that didn't pan out, the hardships their parents lived through, and perhaps most importantly, the memory of their parents and their dreams. The second generation can take risks in a way the first could not. They can calculate risk-reward knowing their core business has delivered a certain rate of return over the course of many decades. That safety net allows for growth potential of exponential order. And oftentimes a family-owned business is the most financially successful under generation two's leadership.

But while generation two is expanding the business from a safe position, generation three does not have the same personal connections to the hard work that was required of their grandparents. Things are more formal now. There are many more employees. Generation three doesn't remember any hardships that hit their family. They've grown up with the knowledge that the business is a success rather than growing up with the dream that it will one day become successful. Their immediate families haven't had to risk much at all, and without that risk, there is less anticipation and reward for generation three. They just don't feel as connected and oftentimes they're interested in pursuing other opportunities. This can be hard for their families. After all, if the grandson wants to pursue painting, which he can afford to do because of the company's success, shouldn't that be considered a win for the family? Generation three is often labeled spoiled, ungrateful, and lazy. This isn't entirely fair. Each generation's attitude toward work is a direct reflection on the stage the family business was at during their upbringing. Generation three was afforded more luxuries—most commonly, education—that generation one never had, so it's not a surprise that they have different goals.

> Generation three is often labeled spoiled, ungrateful,
> and lazy. This isn't entirely fair. Each generation's
> attitude toward work is a direct reflection on the
> stage the family business was at during their
> upbringing.

This model works well when thinking about whether or not to hire an employee's relatives. We all love to do favors, but you must ask yourself who is benefiting most. If your job is to hire the best people, you need to think honestly about this. You may benefit from hiring your boss's daughter. Your boss's daughter may benefit from getting a higher position than she would have if her mom worked elsewhere. And your boss might benefit because she feels good about the fact that her daughter now has her own steady income.

But here's the little-talked-about truth: the kid isn't going to feel good. Even though Greta had the perfect pedigree for the job, she knows her mom helped open the door. And if she's like most children of executives, she may feel like her whole career is due to her mother's success. Even her MBA from Harvard is called into question when she reflects on what she honestly earned on her own accord. This is a tough place to be. Our self-worth is directly linked to our sense of purpose. Our desire to drive impact and be useful is perhaps our most dominant determiner of happiness. If you don't know that you deserve to be at a certain company in a particular job, you will likely feel like a fraud. That is not what you want for your employees. You want them to feel integral to the company's operations, just like generation two. You want them to know that their work matters, that they are useful and necessary.

You will mess up the hire and fuel resentment from other employees if you do not address this elephant in the room. When you're hiring someone with a powerful connection in the business, it is best to address things head-on with both parties.

> ✓ *You will mess up the hire and fuel resentment from*
> ✓ *other employees if you do not address this elephant*
> ✓ *in the room. When you're hiring someone with a*
> ✓ *powerful connection in the business, it is best to*
> ✓ *address things head-on with both parties.*

The hiring manager can always defer to the company's HR guidelines, but in a loaded political environment it might be more prudent to just have a straight talk with the candidate. They are likely more aware of the favor being called in on their behalf than your boss, who thinks because her daughter is qualified, this isn't a big deal. The hiring manager or the HR rep can simply say:

"You have a terrific background and great experience. We would love to have you join the online marketing team, but first let's talk a bit about expectations and contributions. The role you're taking on is critical to the overall operations of this business. You will be a significant person here. But we'd be neglectful not to talk about how your mom is one of the most important people here. She runs the department you'll be working in. This may make other employees feel uncomfortable if they're on a team with you, or if they are your direct manager but your mom's subordinate.

That's just how it goes. But our hope is that talking about all of this will help set clear expectations for you and for your colleagues. We aren't hiring you because of your mother. We've evaluated all of the candidates and think you're the right one for the job. So, let's talk about this. What are some of the things you're thinking about in regards to your job functions and your mother's authority? What are some worries you have? How can we evaluate you for potential promotions in a way that makes you feel confident that you're being assessed on your work and not your genes?"

Coming up with a detailed plan at the beginning can help a lot in the long run. If Greta is as great as her experience suggests, then she is worth investing in. If you can help her feel independently powerful and confident in her abilities, she will become a loyal and hardworking employee. But, if you don't do this, deep in her heart, she will wonder if she's only there because of her mother, and that can lead to resentment, potentially rebellious behavior, or a sense of damaged self-worth for the employee. Our behaviors escalate when we think we're getting away with something because we want to see how far we can push things before we're confronted. That is not what you want happening in your office.

But talking and facilitating open communication can remedy even the most difficult situations.

> ∨   *Our behaviors escalate when we think we're getting*
> ∨   *away with something because we want to see how*
> ∨   *far we can push things before we're confronted.*
> ∨   *That is not what you want happening in your office.*
> ∨   *But talking and facilitating open communication can*
> ∨   *remedy even the most difficult situations.*

Key Takeaways

- Open conversations about expectations are the best protections.
- If the new hire is related to someone else in the business, talk about it after the offer has been made.
- Reassure the person that they will be an asset to the team.
- Provide every new hire with a contact they can communicate with that is not a relative if there is an issue!

SIXTEEN

The Offer
Is Just a Formality

You've screened dozens of resumes, interviewed a handful of candidates, and boiled down your data. You know who you want to hire. Now you need to construct an offer and convince your top candidate that you should be their next employer. This is where the tables might turn if you view this part of the process like closing a sale, which can be a big mistake.

Any insecurities you have about the role, the company, or yourself as a boss will all come pouring out now. Even if you have a stack of well-qualified applicants you can defer to if your first choice passes, you are now the vulnerable one, because you have to open yourself up to rejections.

What if the candidate thinks the salary is too low? What if they need benefits right away and you have a company policy that they need to work for a period of time before the benefits kick in? What if they said they were excited to work in an office, but the role has changed, and the position will become a home-based job?

There are endless reasons why you might feel nervous about offering an applicant the job. And chances are, the smaller the talent pool, or the more limited your resources (time, money, etc.) are, the more stressful this process will be.

That's why it is so, so important to get this last stage of the hiring process right. It is not just a formality, it is potentially the first official interaction the new hire has in their new position with their new employer. That is significant. It sets the stage for the future of the relationship in a significant way.

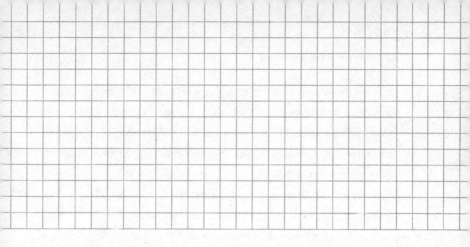

SEVENTEEN

Offer the Moon and Stars to Your Top Candidate

Sam* was desperate for top talent at her biotech start-up. The competition in the valley was fierce, and she knew that word about an opening at Myson would spread quickly. The best and brightest want to be at the best new companies. It was Sam's turn in the spotlight, and her strategy was to swoop up as many talented young people as she could and get the most out of them before the tides turned and the new migration patterns led talent to more desirable opportunities.

With this trend-based talent turnover, there could be long periods of drought where you had to make do with second choices. And all tech entrepreneurs hated those dry patches. Sam's business had been in a drought, and she was starting to feel like Myson would never bounce back. Her new plan was to make the jobs themselves sound like dream opportunities. She hoped word would spread that the potential at Myson was explosive, and that there would soon be a mass exodus from the competition back into her baby.

Sam would never be able to reconcile her vision with reality if she couldn't drum up the talent base she needed.

After several rounds with dozens of interviews, Sam settled on a couple of candidates she really wanted. She sent them all new computers with a note: Your dream job awaits.

The candidates were impressed. They all followed up with a phone call, wanting more details. The proposed salaries were slightly below the most competitive offers, but not far out of range given the end-of-year profit-based bonuses they would be eligible for. But the main draw was the freedom to solve big problems the way each individual saw fit. Start-ups, especially tech start-ups, often tout their respect for individual autonomy. The workspace is designed like a cool lounge, creating a relaxed atmosphere where fun and productivity mingle seamlessly. Employees enjoy unlimited vacation days. They wear what they want. The workforce sets the company's goals. These were all typical perks, and Sam planned to offer them too. Everyone implicitly understood that while all of these practices were interesting ideas, the reality was far from a utopia.

Often the very same companies with unlimited vacation policies fostered a political environment where expectant mothers delivered children and returned to work the following week. Sure, everyone "could" take time off, but no one did because the leadership never did. No low-level coder is going to be the test case for this kind of vacation policy, especially when the higher-ups who enacted it weren't willing to support it in practice. Meanwhile, open-workspace environments have resulted in employees opting to work from home. You don't go to work to hang out: you go to work to be productive, and that can be a challenge when there's a constant ping-pong tournament happening next to your desk. Most workers know these things to be true, but they still assign value to employers who are trying to improve their workplace conditions—even when they don't actually yield results.

When you hire, or when you're hired, the perks of the job should never outweigh the value of the work. No matter how cool the office space is, you aren't going to love being there if you hate your job. For an offer to be enticing, it must be built around the work itself—all the other stuff is icing.

ⅴ *When you hire, or when you're hired, the perks of*
ⅴ *the job should never outweigh the value of the work.*
ⅴ *No matter how cool the office space is, you aren't*
ⅴ *going to love being there if you hate your job.*

Sam was desperate, and when people feel panicked, they aren't very adept at long-term thinking. There was nothing about her hiring strategy that would facilitate long-term success. She was like a vacuum hoping to suck up talent as quickly as she could.

When she talked to the candidates about their potential roles, Sam was intentionally vague. She needed them to work hard once they were onboard, but right now, she was in sales mode, and she was willing to say whatever she could in order to reel them in.

A few of the very best applicants passed on the job because they didn't feel like they understood what was expected of them, and they had other offers with clearly defined roles. But several others eagerly signed on without knowing their day-to-day responsibilities. They'd been excited by the sparkle and glitz of the fame and fortune they'd been promised when all the "work" was done.

When they started, they were trained on systems and protocols and then given assignments. Everything seemed to be going well. But Sam measured individual contributions to her start-up by tying assignments to production scores, based on metrics like how many assignments employees completed, how difficult their tasks were, and whether or not they were able to complete them on time. It was a brilliant scheme from a production perspective, though it was shortsighted because it neglected to recognize a key difference between humans and machines. When machines are given tasks and taught to learn from them, there is no emotional element: a machine will not feel resentful about their workload or as though their work is being taken for granted. Machines won't feel burnt out. They don't require validation.

Sam's system was designed to measure output as if the worker *were* a machine. The individual's score determined their potential bonus, so it had a very significant outcome for each worker. Everyone hated it. There was no autonomy. The only creativity came from the worker's own ability to scheme and calculate where to cut corners. Doing a mediocre job, but turning an assignment in early seemed to earn employees more points than doing a perfect job on an assignment and turning it in on time. Employees spent a lot of time comparing notes to see how they could game Sam's system. And over time, this eroded morale and they were looking for new jobs.

Sam would have been better off being honest about her expectations. She might have gone as far as to explain the systems she had in place and find out who in the talent pool thrived in a deadline-oriented environment. Sam pulled a bait and switch with her employees. She offered them freedom and incentives, but made it nearly impossible for people to reach them. It's the perfect recipe to create discontent among your workforce.

When you're offering employees a job, you want to make sure the job is one they want. They will eventually find out what the job entails, and if it isn't what they thought they signed up for, or if it's not what they want to spend the majority of their time doing, they'll leave and you'll spend more time and money hiring their replacements. It is always best practice to set clear and honest expectations up front. You can be as flexible as you want with the candidate when it comes to how the role is defined, but you must be clear about what you expect from them.

> ∨ *When you're offering employees a job, you want*
> ∨ *to make sure the job is one they want. They will*
> ∨ *eventually find out what the job entails, and if it isn't*
> ∨ *what they thought they signed up for, or if it's not*
> ∨ *what they want to spend the majority of their time*
> ∨ *doing, they'll leave and you'll spend more time and*
> ∨ *money hiring their replacements.*

It's tempting to tell the applicant that everything will be sunshine and roses when they come onboard, but doing so will mean more work for you in the long run.

Key Takeaways

Honesty is the best policy.

- Always answer questions to the best of your ability.
- Consider letting the desired applicant shadow someone in the role they will be taking to make sure they're eager to do the job.
- Set realistic expectations about the workload, the communication after hours, the time-off policies, and any other factors that might come as a surprise to the applicant.
- Remember, as much as you may want them on your team, it will be a big waste of time and money if you hire them, train them, only to have them decide the job is not right for them. Find that out before they start and save everyone!

EIGHTEEN

Do Not Set Clear Expectations

You have the opportunity to set the stage for a successful future if you're clear about the role—what will the new employee be responsible for, who do they report to, what areas of growth may be expected, how long do most people stay in the role and why the candidate was selected for the position, etc.—from the beginning. Contracts serve this purpose in a very formal way, but you can accomplish the same goal by being forthright from the get-go.

All too often, hiring managers don't think the details are important or they are simply focused on bigger issues. And the best way to ensure a new employee adds to your turnover rate is to be less-than-forthcoming about the role, your company's culture, and your expectations.

If Jill* starts a job thinking she can come in at any time wearing whatever she wants, and she isn't sure whom she reports to—directly or otherwise—she may be in for a world of hurt. Showing up to a start-up or a lab in a suit can feel awful, and showing up to an investment bank in sneakers might make someone feel just as out-of-place. When employees feel embarrassed because they're not dressed appropriately—and there is a wide range of what's considered acceptable in the workplace these days—this sting can linger and impact an employee's overall happiness. You might assume that new employees have accumulated a sense of your office culture from their interviews, but this would be wrong. The truth is that most people are nervous during interviews, and much like eyewitnesses to a crime, they may not have picked up very accurate information. It is always best to be super clear. "We have a very casual dress code here. No one ever wears suits, and our sneaker game is fierce."

What if job candidates were able to visit an office and spend time with their potential coworkers, just as prospective undergraduates can visit campuses and interact with current students? Hardly anyone does this, but I'd bet those who do would have a lower turnover rate. You want to make sure that the people you're bringing onboard want to be there. The application and the interview processes are both designed to keep the employer in control, while the offer puts the power in the employee's hands. But if we thought about this as an equal relationship, we would see the value of ensuring that candidates feel as committed to the workplace as their future employer does.

Turnover is one of the biggest liabilities in any business, in every industry. Paying HR reps to screen, interview, and hire is just the tip of the iceberg. Companies invest in their employees every day. Learning job functions, acquiring the necessary skills, building relationships with clients and coworkers—all require the employer to spend time and money helping the employee accomplish their goals. If and when an employee leaves, the employer can evaluate who got more from the initial opportunity. The shorter the relationship, the more the calculation is weighted toward the employee. Companies, firms, hospitals, and schools all have to invest a lot up front.

> ⌄ *If and when an employee leaves, the employer can*
> ⌄ *evaluate who got more from the initial opportunity.*
> ⌄ *The shorter the relationship, the more the calculation*
> ⌄ *is weighted toward the employee.*

Some companies famously offer new employees a couple thousand dollars to leave within the first month of starting! Why would they do this? Because they want to make sure everyone who works there wants to be there. Offering a buyout after a few months of employment gets rid of the employees who aren't happy, who would rather have a big payday, and who are likely going to be less committed in the long run. This approach to hiring is the end product of an analysis that found paying employees to leave saved them money in the long run. It is really important to think about that equation when you're hiring someone and setting the stage for their future with your company.

NINETEEN

It's Totally Fine to Ghost the Applicants You Didn't Hire

Reach out to the candidates you want to hire and make them an offer. Set realistic expectations and then move on. There's no need to follow up with the candidates you didn't hire. If they weren't worthy of an offer, why bother putting any more into the relationship, right?

Wrong!! You must absolutely treat all candidates with respect. The ones that weren't selected are still humans, with emotions, and they're likely waiting to hear back from you—especially people who have come in for interviews and taken time to fill out paperwork, undergone background checks, offered references, or completed any testing. You asked for their time, and they gave it to you: the least you can do in return is let them know that the position has been filled. You can't ghost when you're hiring.

> ∨ *You must absolutely treat all candidates with*
> ∨ *respect. The ones that weren't selected are still*
> ∨ *humans, with emotions, and they're likely waiting to*
> ∨ *hear back from you—especially people who have*
> ∨ *come in for interviews and taken time to fill out*
> ∨ *paperwork, undergone background checks, offered*
> ∨ *references, or completed any testing.*

If extending a little courtesy by reaching out to applicants isn't incentive enough, perhaps you should also consider how small the world is—not to mention your industry, company, or department. As a rule of thumb, imagine you are the candidate—because you will likely one day be on the other side of the table—treat others as you wish to be treated. Hiring is no exception to the Golden Rule.

All too often people will say, "I haven't heard back in a couple of weeks, so I guess I didn't get the job." This is not acceptable. It leaves a nasty impression on the job applicant, especially if they've come in multiple times and completed any testing or mock assignments.

Someday, somewhere, you might want to hire that person and they might remember you as the employer who disregarded them earlier in their career. Or even worse, they might be in a position to hire *you* and decide not to because they felt you were rude.

All it takes is a simple email:

Dear Emily,

We really enjoyed getting to know you and appreciate your time throughout the interview process. We have decided to move forward with another candidate, but you have many of the skills we were looking for, and we wish you the best in your pursuits. We will keep your resume on file for consideration as other positions become available, so please keep us in mind for the future. Thanks again for your interest in [name of business] and for the time you spent on this process.

Best,

Signed by all the people who interacted with the candidate

Because we are busy, we often skip this important step. Many companies have policies preventing employees from disclosing why a candidate wasn't selected or limiting any mention of why their eventual hire was picked for fear of over-sharing, which could unintentionally result in legal action. These policies are up to your individual company, but generally speaking, treating people with respect is the best way to stay out of trouble! If you're not comfortable disclosing specifics about your new hire, you don't need to. The point of this communication is to let the candidates you didn't pick know that the process has ended and that they weren't selected. It gives them some closure and you a chance to offer your sincere thanks for their interest in your organization. Remember, kindness is always queen. Go forth and hire like a pro!

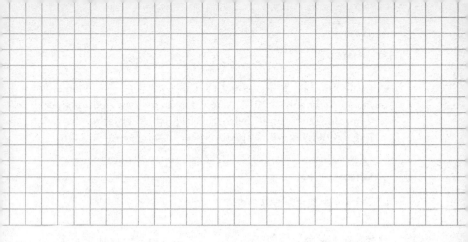

Notes

Chapter 1

1. Byron Auguste, "Low Wage, Not Low Skill: Why Devaluing Our Workers Matters," *Forbes*, February 7, 2019. Accessed at https://www.forbes.com/sites/byronauguste/2019/02/07/low-wage-not-low-skill-why-devaluing-our-workers-matters/#5c37a866716d.

Chapter 2

1. Ariana Tobin, "Employers Used Facebook to Keep Women and Older Workers from Seeing Job Ads. The Federal Government Thinks That's Illegal," ProPublica, September 25, 2019. Accessed at https://www.propublica.org/article/employers-used-facebook-to-keep-women-and-older-workers-from-seeing-job-ads-the-federal-government-thinks-thats-illegal.

2. Princeton University, Engineering School, "Biased Bots: Human Prejudices Sneak Into Artificial Intelligence Systems," Science Daily, April 13, 2017. Accessed at https://www.sciencedaily.com/releases/2017/04/170413141055.htm.

3. Emily Kumler, "Why Artificial Intelligence Is Far Too Human," *Boston Globe*, July 7, 2017. Accessed at https://www.bostonglobe.com/ideas/2017/07/07/why-artificial-intelligence-far-too-human/jvG77QR5xPbpwBL2ApAFAN/story.html.

Chapter 10

1. This is a true, reported story.

Chapter 11

1. This is a true, reported story.

Chapter 12

1. This story has been drastically altered to hide the identities of the real sources; there isn't a reality TV show on the metabolic theory of cancer, but the theory and the work of Otto Warburg and Thomas Seyfried are real and known. I combined the real ideas behind this approach to cancer treatment with a fake show to create a stimulating backdrop for an imaginary show, in order to highlight the lessons learned. Anyone interested in the cancer theory should refer to Thomas Seyfried's book and work for further information.

2. Thomas Seyfried. Accessed at https://tomseyfried.com/.

3. Thomas N. Seyfried, "Cancer as a Mitochondrial Metabolic Disease," *Frontiers in Cell and Developmental Biology* 3:43 (July 2015). Accessed at https://www.ncbi.nlm.nih.gov/pmc/articles/PMC4493566/.

Chapter 14

1. This is a true, reported story.

Chapter 15

1. This is a true, reported story.

Acknowledgments

I'd like to thank Jill Webb, whom I've known only for a short time but whose impact on me has been massive. Thank you for helping me with so many, many projects, including this one. Thank you for putting up with my inability to say "no" to work and making sure we find time for all of it! But, mostly, thank you for being a go-getter who thinks clearly, who is always supportive, and who accomplishes so much. You are brilliant and charming, a potent combination. I feel grateful and lucky to have you by my side. Thank you.

Thank you to Kevin Anderson, who sat across from me on a packed train from Boston to New York where I couldn't help but eavesdrop on his conversation about hiring writers, which led to a conversation between us about his firm and its needs. Months later when he offered me this assignment, it was a reminder that opportunity lurks everywhere. Sometimes we just need to take off our headphones and talk to strangers on trains in order to find our next book deal. Thank you, Kevin, for thinking of me and giving me this opportunity.

—Emily Kumler